Past Masters

Jesus

Jesus wrote no books, but the influence of his life and teaching has been immeasurable. Humphrey Carpenter's account of Jesus is written from the standpoint of a historian coming fresh to the subject without religious preconceptions. And no previous knowledge of Jesus or the Bible on the reader's part is assumed.

How reliable are the Christian 'Gospels' as an account of what Jesus did and said? How different were his ideas from those of his contemporaries? What did Jesus think of himself? Humphrey Carpenter begins his answer to these questions with a survey and evaluation of the evidence on which our knowledge of Jesus is based. He then examines his teaching in some detail, and reveals the perhaps unexpected way in which his message can be said to be original. In conclusion he asks to what extent Jesus's teaching has been followed by the Christian Churches that have claimed to represent him since his death.

This unusually readable book achieves a remarkable degree of objectivity about a subject that is deeply embedded in Western culture. This makes it particularly effective as an introduction, and allows the author to come to some unconventional and original conclusions.

Humphrey Carpenter is best known for his biography of J. R. R. Tolkien, and for his study of the lives and writings of C. S. Lewis and his friends (*The Inklings*). He has also published two books for children, and with his wife Mari Prichard has written a companion to the river Thames. He has recently completed a biography of W. H. Auden, and is currently compiling *The Oxford Companion to Children's Literature*.

Past Masters

AQUINAS Anthony Kenny
DANTE George Holmes
HUME A. J. Ayer
JESUS Humphrey Carpenter
MARX Peter Singer
PASCAL Alban Krailsheimer

Forthcoming

ARISTOTLE Jonathan Barnes
AUGUSTINE Henry Chadwick
BACH Denis Arnold
FRANCIS BACON Anthony Quinton
BAYLE Elisabeth Labrousse
BERGSON Leszek Kolakowski
BERKELEY J. O. Urmson
BURKE C. B. Macpherson
JOSEPH BUTLER R. G. Frey
CARLYLE A. L. Le Quesne
CERVANTES P. E. Russell
COBBETT Raymond Williams
CONFUCIUS Raymond Dawson
COPERNICUS Owen Gingerich
DARWIN Jonathan Howard
DIDEROT Peter France
ENGELS Terrell Carver
ERASMUS James McConica
GALILEO Stillman Drake
GIBBON J. W. Burrow
GODWIN Alan Ryan
GOETHE J. P. Stern
HEGEL Peter Singer
HERZEN Aileen Kelly
HOMER Jasper Griffin
JEFFERSON Jack P. Greene
LAMARCK L. J. Jordanova
LINNAEUS W. T. Stearn
LOCKE John Dunn
MACHIAVELLI Quentin Skinner
MALTHUS Gertrude Himmelfarb
MILL William Thomas
MONTAIGNE Peter Burke
THOMAS MORE Anthony Kenny
MORRIS Peter Stansky
NEWMAN Owen Chadwick
NEWTON P. M. Rattansi
PLATO R. M. Hare
ROUSSEAU John McManners
ST PAUL Tom Mills
SHAKESPEARE Germaine Greer
ADAM SMITH A. W. Coats
TOLSTOY Henry Gifford

and others

Humphrey Carpenter

JESUS

Oxford Toronto Melbourne
OXFORD UNIVERSITY PRESS
1980

Oxford University Press, Walton Street, Oxford OX2 6DP
London Glasgow New York Toronto
Delhi Bombay Calcutta Madras Karachi
Kuala Lumpur Singapore Hong Kong Tokyo
Nairobi Dar es Salaam Cape Town
Melbourne Wellington
and associate companies in
Beirut Berlin Ibadan Mexico City

First published as an Oxford University Press paperback
1980 and simultaneously in a hardback edition
Paperback reprinted with corrections 1980

British Library Cataloguing in Publication Data
Carpenter, Humphrey
Jesus. – (Past masters).
1. Jesus Christ – Teachings
I. Title II. Series
232.9'54 BS2415 79–40974
ISBN 0–19–283016–3

Printed in Great Britain by
Cox & Wyman Ltd, Reading

Preface

This is one of a series of short books on leading intellectual figures of the past, written to give an account of the nature, originality and importance of their ideas. That the person whose life and death gave rise to the founding of Christianity should be chosen as a subject for this series is understandable. But that Jesus should be described as a 'leading intellectual figure of the past' will strike many people as, to say the least, odd. To the Christian Church he is certainly much more than that, while even unbelievers may argue that he was not an 'intellectual figure' at all. Moreover it could be said that to detach the 'ideas' of Jesus from the rest of what the Bible says about him is a mistaken notion.

This book does not try to detach them. But it does examine his teaching in some detail, and tries to determine the character of that teaching by comparing it with the teaching of Jesus's contemporaries. It also attempts to give an account of modern historians' and theologians' views of Jesus and of the Gospels in which his life is recorded. Most of all, it tries to discuss the evidence about him from a historical point of view, without bringing to bear upon it the theological presuppositions of Christianity. If it does not always provide satisfactory answers, it may at least succeed in raising important questions in the reader's mind.

It begins with a brief study of the Gospels as historical evidence. This is for two reasons: first, so that the reader who does not know the New Testament may have a summary of the Gospel traditions about Jesus readily at hand, and second, so as to show the character of the Gospels as historical documents. I hope that even those readers who know the Gospels well may find some fresh things in this part of the book.

I am not a theologian by training, so I have leant very heavily on those whom I have consulted for advice and criticism, especially Tom Mills, Dennis Nineham, and my father, H. J. Carpenter. Henry Hardy of the Oxford University Press has helped me a great deal, and indeed I am grateful to him for asking me to write the book.

Unless otherwise indicated, quotations are taken from the New English Bible, second edition © 1970, by permission of Oxford and Cambridge University Presses. The following abbreviations refer to books of the Bible:

Col.	The Letter of Paul to the Colossians
1 Cor.	The First Letter of Paul to the Corinthians
2 Cor.	The Second Letter of Paul to the Corinthians
Deut.	Deuteronomy
Ex.	Exodus
Gal.	The Letter of Paul to the Galatians
Gen.	Genesis
Is.	Isaiah
Jn.	The Gospel according to John
Lev.	Leviticus
Lk.	The Gospel according to Luke
1 Macc.	The First Book of the Maccabees
Matt.	The Gospel according to Matthew
Mk.	The Gospel according to Mark
Rom.	The Letter of Paul to the Romans
1 Thess.	The First Letter of Paul to the Thessalonians
2 Thess.	The Second Letter of Paul to the Thessalonians

Contents

1 A problem of sources

Jesus did not write any books; or if he did, which seems highly unlikely, they have not survived. This means that an account of his ideas, such as this book is meant to be, faces a special difficulty at the outset. It has to depend for its sources not on his own work, as books on (say) Dante or Pascal or Aquinas can do. but on what he is reported to have said and done. Naturally this introduces an element of unreliability from the start.

And it is not just in the area of his ideas that we are on uncertain ground. Even the simple historical facts about his life are very few. We can, it is true, regard a few things as virtually certain. Jesus was a Jewish religious teacher, and in about A.D. 28–30 he was put to death by crucifixion. When we turn to what happened after that, the facts become more numerous. His followers began to claim that he had risen from the dead and had ascended into heaven, where he had taken his place as the Son of God. Those who held this belief gradually broke away from the main stream of Jewish religion, and came to be known as 'Christians' because of their belief that Jesus was the 'Christ', a Greek word which is the equivalent of the Hebrew 'Messiah' and means 'the anointed one'; the coming of this 'Messiah' had been long expected by Jews. These facts can be deduced from Roman and Jewish writings of the period, which supply enough passing references to the death of Jesus for us to be certain that he really did exist, and was not just (as has occasionally been suggested) a mythical figure invented by Christians. But with regard to what happened before his death, we cannot be at all certain.

In order to find out why this is so, and as a preliminary to our investigation of what may have been the ideas of Jesus – and there must always be some element of 'may have' in it – we need to look at the sources, chiefly the four 'Gospels' found in the Christian Bible, which are Christianity's own account of its founder's life and ideas.* We need to look both at what they say about Jesus

* The Bible is the collection of documents regarded by the Jewish and Christian religions as embodying the word of God. It is divided into the Old Testament, the Apocrypha, and the New Testament. The Old Testament consists of those books recognised by the Jews, chiefly the Law (the first five books of the Old Testament) and the writings of the Prophets. The Christian Church, too, recognises the Old Tes-

and at the ways in which they differ from each other. Then we need to discuss, very briefly, their character as historical documents. After that, we can turn our attention fully to the nature of Jesus's ideas, and their uniqueness and importance.

Mark's Gospel

The four Gospels (the word 'gospel' means 'good news') were written in Greek, probably in the later decades of the first century A.D.; the earliest surviving manuscripts of any substance date from the fourth century, though there are fragments in existence of earlier origin. Of the four, the one entitled 'According to Mark' is both the shortest and that which most scholars believe to have been written first. I will summarise its contents in more detail than those of the other three Gospels, to give a reader not acquainted with the Bible a fairly full idea of the Christian picture of Jesus, and also to show the theme which runs through it. This theme is Mark's concern to answer the question, 'Who was Jesus?'

Mark's opening words provide an answer to the question at once: 'Here begins the Gospel of Jesus Christ the Son of God.' His account of Jesus's life starts with John the Baptist, a roughly-clad preacher, calling on men to be baptised (ritually immersed in water) in the river Jordan in Palestine, as a sign that they have repented of their sins and are forgiven by God. Among those who come to John for this baptism is a man named Jesus from Nazareth in the Palestinian province of Galilee. John baptises Jesus, and the baptism is accompanied by miraculous signs and a voice from heaven saying to Jesus: 'Thou art my Son.' After his baptism, Jesus undergoes some kind of struggle or temptation in a wilderness with Satan the prince of devils, and then returns to his native district preaching the 'gospel' of God. His message is: 'The kingdom of God is upon you; repent, and believe the Gospel.' He gathers a handful of followers, some of them fishermen on the Lake of Galilee, and goes to the town of

---

tament as authoritative, and has added to it a New Testament (consisting chiefly of 'Gospels' and 'Letters') which records the life, death and resurrection of Jesus, and the teaching of Paul and other early Christian preachers. The Apocrypha consists of various books regarded as of more dubious authority than the Old and New Testaments. Unless otherwise stated, all 'books' referred to in the following pages will be found in the Bible, of which many translations are available.

Capernaum where on the Sabbath, the Jewish day of abstention from all work (which fell on every seventh day), he teaches in the synagogue, the local place of worship. In the congregation is a man dominated by an evil spirit or devil which makes him suffer convulsions, and this devil calls out to Jesus: 'What do you want with us, Jesus of Nazareth? Have you come to destroy us [i.e. us devils]? I know you who you are – the Holy One of God.' Jesus tells the devil to be silent and come out of the man, and this happens; the convulsions cease and the man is left in peace.

This is only the first of many such actions that Jesus performs. He heals the sick and drives out devils merely by the force of his word and his touch. At one point he heals a man suffering from leprosy, and this causes his reputation to spread widely so that people come from all quarters for cures and exorcisms. He continues to gather disciples, who join his mission as the result of a single command, 'Follow me'. Among them is Levi, a tax gatherer and hence, because of the dishonesty associated with tax collection at the time, someone considered by pious Jews to be a sinner. The Pharisees, one of the principal Jewish religious factions, disapprove of Jesus's association with such men; and they soon find more in his behaviour that they can criticise. As a God-fearing Jew he is expected to keep the religious Law, the code that rules Jewish life, but he and his disciples are observed one Sabbath plucking ears of corn with which to feed themselves as they walk through a field. The Pharisees point out that this is in effect reaping, an activity forbidden on the Sabbath, to which Jesus replies: 'The Sabbath was made for man and not man for the Sabbath.' Such a high-handed attitude to the Law angers the Pharisees, and as a result of this and similar incidents they and their associates begin plotting to dispose of him.

Mark now describes the content of Jesus's teaching. It is characterised by the use of parables (analogy stories) taken largely from rural life. For example, Jesus tells of a sower who scatters seed, of which some comes to grief but some grows into a rich crop. Although he appears to be talking about the kingdom of God his precise meaning is not clear, and Mark says that Jesus's own disciples are largely puzzled.

Twelve of these disciples have now been appointed to be Jesus's companions. Among them is Simon, to whom Jesus gives the name Peter; also another Simon, who is a member of the Zealots, a political group dedicated to freeing Palestine from Roman control; and Judas Iscariot, who was to be 'the man who betrayed him'. The disciples and Jesus cross the Lake of Galilee by boat. On their journey a storm breaks and they are in peril, but Jesus calmly stands up and tells the wind and water to be still. The storm instantly drops, and the disciples say to one another: 'Who can this be whom even the wind and the sea obey?' Another cause of amazement is the occasion when a large and hungry crowd is plentifully fed by Jesus using only the very small quantity of food there is to be had, five loaves and two fishes. Five thousand people are given enough to eat, and twelve basketfuls of scraps are gathered afterwards. The miracles continue: a blind man is given sight, a deaf man's hearing is restored, and there is widespread curiosity as to who Jesus can be. Eventually he asks his own disciples what they make of his identity, and Peter replies: 'You are the Messiah', that is, the 'anointed one' whom many Jews believed would be sent by God to usher in his 'kingdom' on earth (an idea I will examine later). Jesus tells the disciples to keep this discovery to themselves – in other words, though he does not openly admit that he is the Messiah, he does not deny it. And a few days later three of the disciples realise beyond doubt that this is what he is, for on the top of a mountain they see him miraculously clothed in dazzling white and talking with two great figures from Jewish history, Moses the lawgiver and Elijah the prophet – Elijah was expected to return to earth to announce the arrival of the Messiah.

Yet the Messiah, the inaugurator of God's kingdom on earth, was expected to be a glorious figure, and Jesus is quick to point out that his Messiahship would bring him not glory but suffering. 'He began to teach them that the Son of Man [his own title for himself] had to undergo great sufferings. . . to be put to death, and to rise again three days afterwards. He spoke about it plainly.'

After a time Jesus leaves Galilee and sets out with his disciples for Jerusalem, the capital of the Palestinian province of Judaea and the seat of the great temple which is the centre of Jewish religious life. On the way to Jerusalem he again tells his disciples that he will be arrested and executed, and will rise again, adding: 'For even the Son of Man did not come to be served but to serve, and to surrender his life as a ransom for many.'

Arriving in Jerusalem, Jesus makes a triumphal entry. The crowd cries, 'Hosanna! Blessings on him who comes in the name of the Lord! Blessings on the coming kingdom of our father David!' In Jerusalem he causes a stir in the courtyard of the temple by driving out the traders who have stalls there; he also attracts attention because of his teaching and his disputes with representatives of the two chief religious parties, the Pharisees and Sadducees. Though they are unable to trap him into voicing dangerous opinions, they nevertheless determine to have him arrested. Meanwhile a great religious festival begins, and Jesus and his disciples meet at night for a meal which traditionally opens it. At this meal Jesus takes bread, blesses it, distributes it to the disciples and says: 'Take this: this is my body.' He also takes a cup of wine, and while they are drinking from it he says: 'This is my blood of the Covenant, shed for many.' (The 'Covenant' was God's promise to the Jews that they were to be his specially favoured people providing they kept his Law.) Jesus then leads his disciples out on to the Mount of Olives, and there, while he is praying, he is arrested by an armed crowd sent by the chief priests and their associates and guided by Jesus's own disciple Judas, who betrays him with a kiss. Jesus is seized and led to the High Priest's house.

There follows an interrogation at which the High Priest tries to find enough evidence against Jesus to warrant a death sentence. Jesus himself keeps silent until the High Priest asks him: 'Are you the Messiah, the Son of the Blessed One?' Jesus says: 'I am; and you will see the Son of Man seated on the right hand of God and coming with the clouds of heaven.' These words recall the seventh chapter of the prophetic book of Daniel, where the Son of Man is a heavenly being, the lieutenant of God; it is prophesied that he will come 'with the clouds of heaven' and be given a glorious rule over all the earth. This heavenly figure is what Jesus now claims to be, and the High Priest responds by accusing him of blasphemy, and calls for his death. But the Jewish authorities (it seems) do not have the power to carry out this death sentence, for they now hand Jesus over to Pilate, the Roman governor, who himself questions Jesus, asking him: 'Are you the king of the Jews?' Jesus replies ambiguously: 'The words are yours', and Pilate is unable to make him answer any further questions. Eventually he confirms the death sentence, and sends Jesus to be crucified, this being the method of execution which Roman law prescribed at the time. Jesus is mocked and beaten by the Roman soldiers, and is taken to the place of execution and fastened to a wooden cross. After hanging from it for six hours he dies, and a Roman centurion who has watched him and heard his last prayers declares: 'Truly this man was a son of God.'

Mark now tells how, thanks to the intervention of a wealthy Jew, Jesus's body is interred in a tomb cut out of rock. Two days later, when the Sabbath is over, three women followers of Jesus come to the tomb to anoint his body. They find that the huge stone which sealed the grave has been rolled away, and they see a young man dressed in white who says: 'He is risen; he is not here; look, there is the place where they laid him.' The women are ordered to tell the disciples that Jesus will go on before them into Galilee, where they will see him. 'Then', Mark continues, 'they went out and ran away from the tomb, beside themselves with terror. They said nothing to anybody, for they were afraid.'

Here, and very abruptly, the earliest manuscripts of Mark's Gospel came to an end. The paragraphs which follow in most printed versions are unanimously regarded as the work of a later writer. These paragraphs tell how the risen Jesus appeared to his disciples, and was then taken up into heaven to be seated 'at the right hand of God'. This extension to the original text seems to have been copied from the other Gospels. But it does show that from an early stage Mark's readers were puzzled by the abrupt ending of his narrative, and felt that they must continue the story to what they regarded as its proper conclusion.

This, then, is in very abbreviated form the outline of Mark's Gospel. As that Gospel forms the basis of two of the others, we need not look at them in so much detail, but need only note their most obvious differences from Mark.

Matthew's Gospel

Of the remaining three Gospels, that entitled 'According to Matthew' is the one with the most resemblance to Mark. Nine-tenths of Mark's narrative is found in it, and it includes just over half of Mark's actual words. Clearly one of them had copied from the other, and though the question is still open to discussion the usual view is that Matthew used Mark. But he also used a great deal of material which Mark either did not know or decided not to incorporate.

Mark gave no account of Jesus's origins or ancestry, but Matthew begins with a full genealogy. According to this, Jesus had no ordinary list of ancestors: Matthew traces his descent back through twenty-eight generations to David, the most celebrated king in Jewish history, and through another fourteen to Abraham, the patriarch from whom all Jews were believed to be descended. He then explains that while this accounts for the origins of Jesus's nominal father, Joseph, the truth is that Jesus was not the physical son of Joseph at all, but was conceived while his mother was a virgin, as the result of a direct act of God— 'Before their marriage she found that she was with child by the Holy Spirit.' This happened, says Matthew, in order to fulfil the ancient prophecy, 'The virgin will conceive and bear a son.'[3] (The source of this prophecy is the seventh chapter of the prophetic book of Isaiah, and modern commentators point out that 'virgin' is actually a mistranslation, found in the Greek text which Matthew used, for the original Hebrew which meant 'young woman'.)

Matthew says Jesus was born at Bethlehem in Judaea 'during the reign of Herod'. He means Herod I, who ruled Palestine as a puppet-king under the Romans and who died in 4 B.C. As to Bethlehem, Matthew explains that Jesus's birth there fulfils the prophecy, 'Bethlehem in the land of Judah ... out of you shall come a leader to be the shepherd of my people Israel' – an adaptation of verses from the fifth chapter of the book of Micah. Matthew no doubt also had in mind that Bethlehem was the home town of King David.

Matthew tells how after the birth of Jesus a group of 'magi', which means either wise men or magicians (or both), come to visit the child, being led to him by a moving star. Because of their journey, Herod learns of the birth of this child 'who is born to be King of the Jews', and is so perturbed that he orders the massacre of all infants in the Bethlehem district. But Jesus escapes death because Joseph is warned in a dream to flee with the child and its mother into Egypt, and stay there until Herod's death. This, says Matthew, 'was to fulfil what the Lord had declared through the prophet: "I called my son out of Egypt."' Similarly, Matthew sees the slaughter of the innocent Bethlehem children as fulfilling the words of the prophet Jeremiah, 'Rachel weeping for her children'.

A modern reader will probably be intrigued by these frequent declarations by Matthew that events in Jesus's life are fulfilments of prophecies, are indeed taking place *in order* to fulfil those prophecies. This seemingly odd notion is actually quite in keeping with Jewish thought, for it was a fundamental belief that nothing of importance could happen which had not been promised by God and foretold in those writings now known as the Old Testament. Because they believed this, Jewish writers were constantly searching the Old Testament for sayings which could be interpreted as prefiguring recent events. This sometimes led to the assumption that those events had taken place so that the prophecies might be fulfilled. Indeed in a case such as Herod's supposed slaughter of the children, which is not recorded in any other source, we may suspect that the existence of the prophecy led to the invention of the event.

Although Matthew reports that Jesus was born in Bethlehem he knows of the tradition that he came from Nazareth in Galilee, and he explains this by saying that Joseph was warned not to return to Judaea and took the family to Nazareth instead. Even here Matthew adds: 'This was to fulfil the words spoken through the prophet: "He shall be called a Nazarene." ' As it happens, on this occasion no such prophecy can be traced; perhaps here Matthew, faced with the certainty of the event, has invented the prophecy.

Matthew now takes up the narrative which begins Mark's Gospel, the baptism of Jesus by John the Baptist. Then comes the temptation of Jesus in the wilderness by Satan, mentioned only briefly by Mark. Matthew tells the story in much greater detail. After this he recounts the opening of Jesus's ministry, and makes his first major incident a great sermon preached by Jesus. There is nothing like the 'Sermon on the Mount', as it is usually called from the fact that it is preached on a hilltop, in Mark's Gospel. When Mark records Jesus's teaching he concentrates almost entirely on parables and does not portray Jesus as delivering sets of explicit moral precepts. But the Sermon in Matthew's Gospel is not a parable, though parables and colourful imagery are used within it; it is direct and explicit moral teaching. This raises the question of how it compares with the moral precepts laid down by the Law of Moses, the code of Judaism, and Jesus himself answers that question in the Sermon when he says: 'Do not suppose that I have come to abolish the Law . . . I did not come to abolish, but to complete.' We shall see later precisely what Jesus seems to mean by this.

At the conclusion of the Sermon, Matthew takes up the narrative of Jesus's healing, exorcising and preaching in Galilee, and many of the events that he describes are also found in Mark's Gospel. But they do not always appear at the same point in the story, and there is also a good deal of material in Matthew not found in Mark. This new material is sometimes a longer version of something found briefly in Mark; for instance, where Mark has a few sentences in which Jesus gives a 'mission charge' to his disciples, telling them how to conduct themselves when they travel about preaching and healing, Matthew has a much longer speech in which Jesus, besides giving the disciples practical instructions, warns them about the persecutions they will suffer and exhorts them to carry out their work fearlessly. Matthew also records a number of parables and sayings of Jesus not found in Mark. And there is another more subtle way in which his text differs from Mark's: he shows a concern not found in Mark to relate Jesus's teaching to Jewish religion, showing in what manner it 'completes' the Law.

Despite the differences between the texts of Mark and Matthew the two do present very much the same story, especially in their account of the 'Passion', the trial and execution of Jesus and the events that immediately precede and follow it. But there is one significant difference. When the High Priest asks Jesus if he claims to be the Messiah, the Son of God, Jesus answers not 'I am' as in Mark but 'The words are yours' – that is, you have said it, not me, an ambiguous reply such as Jesus gives Pilate in Mark.

After the death and burial of Jesus the women (in Matthew's version) come to the tomb, see the figure in white, and soon afterwards are met by Jesus himself. He tells them: 'Go and take word to my brothers that they are to leave for Galilee. They will see me there.' The women spread the news of his resurrection, and meanwhile, when the news gets out that his tomb is empty, the Jewish religious authorities spread the rumour that the disciples themselves stole the body. The disciples meet Jesus on a mountain in Galilee, where he tells them: 'go forth therefore and make all nations my disciples; baptise men everywhere in the name of the Father and the Son and the Holy Spirit, and teach them to observe all that I have commanded you. And be assured, I am with you always, to the end of time.' With these words Matthew's Gospel ends.

Luke's Gospel

The author to Theophilus: Many writers have undertaken to draw up an account of the events that have happened among us, following the traditions handed down to us by the original eyewitnesses and servants of the Gospel. And so I in my turn, your Excellency, as one who had gone over the whole course of these events in detail, have decided to write a connected narrative for you, so as to give you authentic knowledge about the matters of which you have been informed.

Suddenly we are in a different world. Mark and Matthew have little pretension to literary style. Their Gospels are proclamations of Jesus's miraculous nature and his great power and authority, written with little thought of their own roles as authors. But at the head of the Gospel 'According to Luke' we find an urbane, almost suave introduction, a dedication to a noble patron.

This impression is confirmed by the opening of the narrative, for Luke begins his story more subtly than do Mark or

Matthew. The first figure to appear in it is Zechariah, an elderly priest whose ageing and barren wife is miraculously made fertile, so that the couple become the parents of John the Baptist. Zechariah's wife Elizabeth is kinswoman to Mary, who is betrothed to Joseph of Nazareth in Galilee, and the miraculous birth of John is paralleled by Mary's even more remarkable virginal conception of Jesus, which is announced to her by the angel Gabriel. In this episode Luke demonstrates that he has a fine taste in poetry, for Mary's lyrical response to the angel's message ('Tell out, my soul, the greatness of the Lord') is in literary terms far beyond anything attempted by Mark or Matthew. And it is equalled by the hymns in which Zechariah greets the birth of his son John, and Simeon, a devout man of Jerusalem, hails the child Jesus as the promised Messiah.

If Luke is a poet he is also a historian. Faced with the problem of explaining how Jesus was said to have been born in Bethlehem but was known to have lived in Nazareth, he adopts an ingenious course. Matthew said that Jesus's parents fled from Bethlehem because of the threat from Herod, but Luke apparently knows nothing of this, or if he does he ignores it. He takes up the point of Joseph's Davidic ancestry, and says that though Joseph lived in Nazareth he was obliged to journey with his wife to Bethlehem, the home town of the Davidic family, to register there for a census. Luke knows that this census was a historical event: he says it 'was the first registration of its kind; it took place when Quirinius was governor of Syria'. (Actually, though there was indeed a census during Quirinius's governorship, it was not held until A.D. 6–7, which does not tally with Luke's statement that Jesus was born 'in the days of Herod', for Herod died in 4 B.C.)

Luke's artistry is evident too in his narrative of Jesus's birth. Arriving in Bethlehem, Joseph and his wife find no room to lodge in, so Jesus is born in a stable manger. This vivid detail is not found in Matthew; neither is the visit which Luke describes of a band of shepherds who come to see the new-born child. So his nativity story is almost entirely different from Matthew's, though the two are commonly fused to give the traditional Christmas story. Luke also seems to realise, with a historian's and storyteller's instinct, the enormous gap between the birth of Jesus and his baptism; he alone fills this gap with a story of Jesus growing 'big and strong and full of wisdom,' and at the age of twelve putting a series of brilliant questions to the religious teachers in the temple at Jerusalem. And when he at last takes up the narrative of Jesus's baptism he sets that too in a historical perspective: he says it took place 'in the fifteenth year of the Emperor Tiberius, when Pontius Pilate was governor of Judaea'.

And then suddenly Luke begins to be a disappointment, at least for the reader who has expected the narrative to go on flowing as easily as this. For when he takes up the narrative that we find in Mark and Matthew he often seems to be losing his grip as a historian-storyteller-poet. It is not that he is any worse at narrating the chief events of Jesus's Galilean ministry than are Mark and Matthew; it is simply that he is no better. The literary promise of the early part of his story is not fulfilled. Instead of sustaining an easy flow he opts for the apparently rather haphazard list of events that is found in Mark and Matthew. On the other hand his narrative does differ considerably from theirs. For example he places the great Sermon given by Jesus much later in the story than does Matthew (and it is given on a plain rather than on a mountain) and his text of the Sermon differs quite substantially from Matthew's. He uses many fewer of the actual words of Mark's Gospel than does Matthew. Moreover there is a long section of his Gospel which contains incidents and sayings not found in Mark or Matthew.

His narrative of the 'Passion' of Jesus is much the same as Mark's and Matthew's, but his account of the resurrection is very different. The women at the tomb see the risen Jesus himself, and tell the other disciples what has happened. The scene then changes to the road leading from Jerusalem to a village named Emmaus, along which two followers of Jesus are walking and discussing what has happened. A stranger joins them, and they tell him about the death of Jesus and the rumour of his resurrection, which they can scarcely believe. He in reply expounds to them how the raising of Jesus from the dead was foretold by the prophets. They reach their destination and invite him to eat with them, and as he says a blessing and breaks the bread they recognise him as Jesus himself. At this he vanishes, and they immediately return to Jerusalem and tell the others what has happened. While they are talking about it, Jesus is suddenly standing among them. He tells them that he is no ghost but flesh and blood, and they give him food, which he eats. He then leads them out of the city to the village of Bethany and blesses them, and in the act of so doing he departs from them and (it is implied) ascends into heaven. 'And they returned to Jerusalem with great joy,' concludes Luke, 'and spent all their time in the temple praising God.' Actually Luke did not regard this as the end, not if (as seems to be the case) he was also the author of the 'Acts of the

Apostles'; for that other New Testament book takes up the story at the point where Luke's Gospel ends, and tells how the Spirit of God descended on the disciples, and they began their task of preaching the message of Jesus to the world.

Luke, then, is something of a puzzle, by turns literary and unsophisticated, close to Mark and Matthew and then departing radically from them. But he still bears much more resemblance to them than does the fourth Gospel.

John's Gospel

'When all things began, the Word already was. The Word dwelt with God, and what God was, the Word was.' So opens the resounding prologue to the Gospel entitled 'According to John'.

The Gospels of Mark, Matthew and Luke are commonly referred to by the title 'synoptic', because despite their great differences from each other the wording of all three is sufficiently identical to be usefully set out in the parallel columns of a 'synopsis'. But John's Gospel does not fit into this pattern. A few of the incidents from the 'Synoptics' turn up in his narrative, and his account of the 'Passion' is substantially the same, but there the resemblance ends. It is not merely that he has different miracle stories and teachings in his account of Jesus's life; his whole portrait of Jesus is based on a different presupposition. He regards Jesus as no less than a manifestation in human flesh of the 'Word' of God, pre-existent since before the beginning of creation. This is expressed in John's prologue, which comes to its climax with the dramatic words 'So the Word became flesh; he came to dwell among us.'

John does not give any account of the birth of Jesus, but begins his narrative with the baptism by John the Baptist. He then records a series of miracles and sayings of Jesus, but both show marked differences from those in the Synoptics. The first miracle is not a healing, but the turning by Jesus of water into wine at a wedding-feast. John says that this was the first of Jesus's 'signs'. What he means by this becomes more clear as his Gospel proceeds. To him, the miraculous actions of Jesus are not simply (as they usually are to the Synoptics) wonderful deeds demonstrating the overwhelming authority from God which Jesus possesses, but actions which often have a distinct symbolic meaning. For example, the turning of water into wine means that, just as the wedding party's supply of somewhat inferior wine eventually ran out and was replaced by Jesus's miraculous and splendid vintage, so the Law which governed Jewish life for centuries has outworn its usefulness and is now replaced by the new and better 'wine', the salvation which Jesus brings. And if this interpretation seems forced, it should be noted that in Jewish rabbinical literature wine is regularly used as a symbol for the Law – and incidentally marriage is a common Old Testament metaphor for God's relationship to Israel. Such secondary interpretation of Jesus's actions is not entirely foreign to the Synoptics, but John is more conscious of it, and it governs his selection of incidents.

The sayings of Jesus recorded in John's Gospel are remarkably different from those in the Synoptics. The Jesus of the Synoptics is colourful in his speech and capable of dealing with tricky questions by means, if necessary, of equally tricky answers. He is not so much concerned with his own nature and role as with the immediate demands of the 'kingdom of God', demands which make the question of his own personality largely irrelevant. When he does speak of himself it is usually in the third person, as 'the Son of Man'. But the Jesus of John's Gospel is not like this at all. He scarcely ever teaches in the lively parables which are so typical of the Synoptics, nor does he habitually call himself the Son of Man; he is simply 'the Son', the only Son of God. Moreover he is much more like God than man, a deity clothed in human flesh but still undoubtedly a deity. And, after the marked lack of interest in his own personality shown by the Jesus of the Sypnotic Gospels, it is extraordinary to note how much of John's text is taken up by Jesus's speeches about himself. 'I am the light of the world . . . I am the good shepherd . . . I am the bread of life.' With these and other images he begins the great discourses so typical of him in this Gospel, discourses which are great sermons about man's relationship to God through Jesus himself, and in which the word 'I' plays a great part.

Nor is it only the colour of the Synoptics which is missing in John's portrait of Jesus. Many of the central ideas are not there either. As the modern theologian John Knox has put it, in his book *The Death of Christ*:

> The Christ of the Fourth Gospel is almost entirely preoccupied with his own significance to the complete neglect of the great themes of the righteous will, the abounding goodness, and the imminent kingdom of God which dominate and give their distinctive character to the utterances of Jesus in the other Gospels.

This means that on the one hand John provides a peculiarly rich source of ideas about the nature of Jesus as 'Christ' and 'Son of

God': the Christian religion's own thought about Jesus's nature undoubtedly owes more to John that it does to the Synoptics. On the other hand John's portrait has supplied comparatively little to historians' understanding of Jesus as a man. It is generally considered that his Gospel is a work of spiritual reflection rather than of reliable history, and in this book it will be to the Synoptics that we shall usually turn for our information about Jesus, rather than to John.

Other sources

These four Gospels are the main sources of information about the life of Jesus, but there are other documents which ought to be mentioned very briefly. Most notable among these is a passage in the first Letter to the Corinthians by the early Christian preacher Paul of Tarsus. This was probably written quite a lot earlier than the Gospels, for Paul became a Christian only a few years after the death of Jesus, whereas the Gospels seem to have originated some time later. In the fifteenth chapter of this Letter he writes:

> . . . I handed on to you the facts which had been imparted to me: that Christ died for our sins, in accordance with the scriptures; that he was buried; that he was raised to life on the third day, according to the scriptures; and that he appeared to Cephas [Paul's name for Peter], and afterwards to the Twelve. Then he appeared to over five hundred of our brothers at once, most of whom are still alive, though some have died. Then he appeared to James, and afterwards to all the apostles.
>
> In the end he appeared even to me. (1 Cor. 15. 3–8)

This shows that from a very early stage Christianity was based on the death and resurrection of an actual person, but of course it tells us nothing about what Jesus said and did in his lifetime. Indeed in all of Paul's writings there are only two passages which give us any explicit information about the historical Jesus. The first is in the context of Paul's discussion of marriage, where he says: 'A wife must not separate herself from her husband', and declares that this ruling 'is not mine but the Lord's', that is Jesus's (1 Cor. 7.10). The second comes when he is discussing how the congregation to whom he is writing should celebrate the 'Lord's Supper', the ritual meal which was a regular activity from the beginning of Christianity. Paul reminds them that this meal is a tradition which came directly from Jesus:

> . . . the Lord Jesus, on the night of his arrest, took bread and, after giving thanks to God, broke it and said. 'This is my body, which is for

you; do this as a memorial of me.' In the same way, he took the cup after Supper, and said: 'This cup is the new covenant sealed by my blood. Whenever you drink it, do this as a memorial of me.' (1 Cor. 11. 23–6)

And that is all Paul has to tell us about the historical Jesus. This is not as strange as it may seem, because from its beginnings Christianity regarded Jesus not so much as a person in the past as a living presence; so that Paul's view of Jesus is set, so to speak, in the present tense. Moreover Paul, himself a great preacher, was less concerned to record stories about the life of Jesus (which his congregations probably already knew) than to emphasise the meaning of Christianity. Nevertheless it is frustrating that one who was so close to the historical facts tells us so little about them.

Apart from the Gospels of Mark, Matthew, Luke and John and the Letters of Paul, all of which are to be found in that part of the Bible known as the New Testament, there are a number of other early accounts of Jesus's life which have survived. Several of these other Gospels represent traditions about him which were preserved by branches of Christianity whose doctrines differed from the main stream. For example there is the 'Gospel of the Egyptians', which represents Jesus's purpose as being to destroy 'the works of the female', by which is apparently meant the process of reproduction. Another fragment, the so-called 'Secret Gospel of Mark', portrays Jesus as initiating his disciples privately into some kind of sexual rites, while the 'Gospel of the Ebionites' says he made it his aim to terminate all sacrifices in the temple of Jerusalem. It is impossible to take this kind of thing seriously unless one is prepared to discount the whole body of New Testament writings about Jesus. More in harmony with the New Testament tradition are the Gospels known as 'Hebrews', 'Peter', and 'Thomas'. But the first two, of which only fragments exist, seem to be no more than modifications of the Synoptic Gospels, while the third, which is complete, does contain sayings of Jesus not found elsewhere but appears to be merely an imaginative expression of the Synoptics and not to be based on first-hand traditions.

So in our investigation of the life and ideas of Jesus we are left with the four Gospels of the New Testament as our principal sources. How are we to regard them?

The quest for the historical Jesus

The Gospels themselves imply that they are eyewitness reports.

Indeed the Gospel of John actually claims to be the work of an eyewitness, who has usually been identified with John the son of Zebedee, one of Jesus's twelve disciples. As for Luke's Gospel, its author does not say he observed its events himself, but tells us he bases his accounts on traditions handed down by those who did. (Luke himself has been popularly identified with Luke the physician, the travelling companion of Paul, though this tradition is now widely regarded as wrong.) The other two Gospels make no statement about their own authenticity, but at quite an early date traditions grew up about them. A second-century church leader in Asia Minor named Papias explained Mark's Gospel as originating in the reminiscences of the disciple Peter, who dictated them to a follower named Mark. This soon became the general belief, as did the notion that Matthew's Gospel was the work of the tax-gatherer disciple who is called 'Levi' in Mark but 'Matthew' in Matthew.

Once the early Church had made up its mind to accept these four Gospels as authentic and to reject all others, the question of their reliability was not raised for many centuries. Medieval Christians did not concern themselves with it, and even at the Reformation the issue was scarcely touched on, though the foundations of later investigation were laid by Luther's insistence that the Bible rather than the Church was the real source of the word of God. This led to a more thorough study of what the Bible had originally meant; meanwhile such scholars as Erasmus had begun to investigate the original Greek texts of the Gospels. But it was not until the eighteenth century that it was admitted that the Bible could contradict itself, and might reflect very different points of view. With this came the beginning of real historical investigation.

The fact that Matthew, Mark and Luke tell roughly the same story (though with considerable variations) led the early investigators to look for some kind of 'primal Gospel' which it was supposed must lie behind them all; meanwhile John's very different Gospel was quietly set aside, and the question of its historicity was not discussed. First results for the 'primal Gospel' suggested that Matthew's account was the earliest of the three Synoptics to be written, a view which the early Church had held. But by the mid-nineteenth century the growth of Gospel criticism showed that Mark's account almost certainly preceded the other two, and that Matthew and Luke drew upon it, augmenting their narratives with material presumably based on another tradition about Jesus, to which scholars affixed the name 'Q', perhaps from the German *Quelle*, meaning 'source'.

This led to the assumption that Mark's account of Jesus must be the 'primal Gospel' which everyone was looking for. But further study showed that this assumption presented grave difficulties. If Mark was pure history, it was history of a very odd kind. A great deal was lacking: there was no information about Jesus's birth or early life, and no real explanations of his character and motives. Moreover, while there was no lack of incidents in the narrative, everything was presented as happening in quick succession, so that if it all took place just as Mark said it did the whole series of events would only occupy a few weeks. When this was realised by nineteenth-century historians there were two results.

The first was that certain people tried to fill the gaps in Mark's narrative by writing conjectural biographies of Jesus, extraordinary books whose contents are summarised in Albert Schweitzer's *The Quest of the Historical Jesus*, and which reflect not so much the personality of Jesus as those of their authors. Among these books were rationalistic attempts to prove that the miracles were not miraculous at all but merely ordinary events misinterpreted by the disciples; allegations that Jesus was a member of a religious secret society which stage-managed (and faked) his death and resurrection; and highly romantic Lives of Jesus whose saccharine sweetness appealed to a vast public. Writings like these were much in vogue for some years – and indeed the same sort of thing is sometimes published today. Needless to say they contribute nothing to the historian's knowledge of Jesus.

The second result of discovering Mark's inadequacy as a biographer of Jesus was that the whole nature of his Gospel was called into question; and a careful study of the original Greek text eventually led to the conclusion that his narrative had been put together from a large number of originally independent stories about Jesus. What Mark himself had done was to assemble these stories into a continuous narrative, providing linking passages where necessary. His Gospel was therefore in no sense a biography, but a loosely-knit collection of independant items. This did not automatically make it less reliable as history. It will be remembered that the early Church believed that Mark had written at the dictation of Jesus's disciple Peter; so could not the disjointed nature of Mark's materials be explained as the fragmentary reminiscences of an old man? Maybe, and some would still hold this view; but there is actually very little in the Gospel which bears the character of an eyewitness's memories. Colourful details are largely lacking, and most events are described very barely, not at all as somebody who had been there might have reported them. Moreover there are many sayings ascribed to Jesus which could only have come from his lips if he had foreseen not just the precise circumstances of his death and resurrection but also the growth of a Church which would worship him, and which would in turn itself suffer persecutions for its beliefs. If we do not choose to accept this prophetic element at face value, we may regard this as an indication that Mark's Gospel was not the individual memory of an eyewitness but a general tradition about Jesus preserved corporately in the early Church, a tradition, moreover, that had been embroidered upon by those who preserved it.

These conclusions were reached soon after the 1914–18 war by a group of biblical scholars known as Form-critics, because of their attention to the detailed literary form of the Gospel materials. The Form-critics' work predictably aroused opposition from more conservative quarters, and this opposition was strengthened by the fact that the Form-critics often exaggerated; for example, they tended to assume that because something *could* have been invented by the early Church then it undoubtedly *had* been. However, the general conclusions of this critical school gradually came to be accepted even in more conservative circles.

What then is the present-day historian's attitude to the Gospels as source material? He will begin by considering Mark, since his is generally agreed to be the earliest Gospel and closest to the original traditions about Jesus. If he has a poor opinion of the accuracy of human memory in general and of a corporate memory (such as the early Church must have used to retain these traditions) in particular, he will be sceptical about Mark's chances of recording the truth. This scepticism will be increased if he is inclined to believe (with most New Testament scholars) that Mark's Gospel was not written down until several decades after the death of Jesus, perhaps between A.D. 65 and 75. And if the historian accepts that Christians would at a very early stage freely elaborate, albeit unconsciously, what had been handed down to them, so as to produce a whole new series of traditions about Jesus, then he will again be sceptical about the accuracy of Mark. If on the other hand he believes that Christians' devotion to the memory of Jesus would make them scrupulous in preserving traditions accurately, and that any invention or elaboration of those traditions would be discouraged, then he will probably allow Mark's Gospel a higher degree of historicity. Perhaps if he is wise he will compromise, for it is after all hard to imagine that this earliest Gospel does not preserve something of the impact that Jesus really made, while at the same time it is unrealistic to suppose that much inaccuracy and departure from historical truth did not occur as a result of the oral transmission of memories from one person to another. Finally, he will take account of the fact that Mark's Gospel, like the other three, was written not simply to inform, but to preach. It is didactic writing, and this influences the selection and presentation of its contents.

But what about the historian's attitude to Matthew and Luke? The view of most biblical scholars is still that the other two Synoptic Gospels used the hypothetical source 'Q', which may have been either a written document or an oral tradition, for much of the material that they did not derive from Mark. But if 'Q' was a document it has disappeared, and when it is conjecturally reconstructed it looks rather an odd piece of work, with no real narrative shape. Moreover if it really did exist it seems that Matthew and Luke knew quite different versions of it, because they used its material very differently. Not surprisingly some discount its existence, and prefer the theory that Luke's resemblances to Matthew are not the product of their using a common source but of Luke's having a copy of Matthew's Gospel in front of him when he wrote.

Where then did Matthew get the material that he did not draw from Mark? And why if Luke copied from Matthew did he make so many changes in the narrative? One explanation has recently been offered which accounts for all this. This is that Matthew wrote a free meditation on what he found in Mark; he took Mark's basic outline and most of his details, but altered where he thought fit, and also invented freely to fill out his account of Jesus to his satisfaction. In the same way Luke based his text on Matthew, but he too invented freely and changed Matthew's narrative when he wanted to.

There is a good deal to support this view. All is explained quite simply without reference to hypothetical sources. But could Matthew and Luke really have dared to invent so much? The New Testament critics who believe they could, cite the long established Jewish practice of *midrash* or free improvisation around sacred themes, a practice which certainly lies behind the composition of many of the Old Testament stories, and suggest that

Matthew and Luke as devout Christians in the Jewish tradition would certainly have felt free to compose *midrash* about Jesus. So far this view (which could, of course, be extended even to Mark's Gospel) has not received much support, but it ought to be kept in mind as a possibility. If it is true, then of course Matthew's and Luke's Gospels are totally unhistorical when they depart from Mark – or at least they can be no more than a reflection of Jesus's general impact, and not a record of what he actually said and did.

As for John's Gospel, the historian will probably regard it as the product not so much of historical tradition as of spiritual reflection. At the same time he will perhaps allow that it may contain a few real historical details. He will certainly accept that it records the Church's beliefs about Jesus, as they developed in later decades after Jesus's death.

Whether the Gospels are history or invention they are virtually our only sources for an examination of the life and teaching of Jesus, so that if we reject them we are left with nothing at all. A proper course is therefore not to dismiss them out of hand but to use them with caution, often very great caution, as we set out on our own quest for the historical Jesus.

2 'Jesus came from Nazareth in Galilee'

Jesus was certainly called 'Jesus'. The name was so common that the early Church would not have used it of him had it not been his real name. To be strictly accurate, 'Jesus' is the Greek form. The Hebrew original was 'Jeshua', which (like 'Joshua') was a shortened form of 'Jehoshua', meaning 'he whose salvation is God'.

The Gospels give us two sets of information about Jesus's origins. Mark says he came from Nazareth in Galilee, and tells us that in his home town Jesus was referred to as 'the carpenter, the son of Mary, the brother of James and Joseph and Judas and Simon', mentioning that he had sisters too (Mk. 6. 3). Matthew and Luke add to this; they tell us that Jesus was born in Bethlehem, that his nominal father's name was Joseph, and that his mother became pregnant while still a virgin, so that the child was really fathered by God. How we treat this tradition of the virgin birth will depend on our theological views. As to the notion that Jesus was born in Bethlehem, though this may have been simply a conjecture because Bethlehem was David's home town, it could of course be a historical fact. Galilee, on the other hand, remains unchallenged as the place where Jesus was brought up. 'Jesus came from Nazareth in Galilee and was baptised in the Jordan by John', says Mark (1. 9), and there seems to be no reason to doubt the implication that Nazareth was Jesus's home at the time.

Galilee of the Gentiles

Galilee was the name given to a province in the north of Palestine. Its economy was based on agriculture – the soil was highly fertile – and on fishing in the Lake of Galilee, through which the river Jordan flowed south. About a thousand years before the birth of Jesus, Galilee had been part of the powerful Jewish kingdom of David. But after the death of David's son and successor Solomon this kingdom was divided once again into the two states of Israel and Judah, its original components. Galilee became part of Israel, the northern state. After a period of peace, in the eighth century B.C. this territory fell to the Assyrians, and its people lost their Israelite identity. The majority of them ceased to worship Yahweh the God of Israel, and turned instead to the Ba'als or heathen deities whose fertility cults had long been popular in the eastern Mediterranean.

The southern state of Judah had Jerusalem, the seat of the great temple built by Solomon for the worship of Yahweh, as its capital. Eventually this kingdom, too, fell to invaders. It was captured by the Babylonians in 587 B.C., and its principal inhabitants were taken in bondage to Babylon. Their captivity there lasted for fifty years, and when they were eventually freed and could return to Judah they were unable to rebuild a nation of any great power. Meanwhile Galilee and the other northern territories that had once been part of the kingdom of David remained in 'Gentile' or non-Jewish hands.

Not until little more than a hundred years before the birth of Jesus did this picture change. In the second century B.C. the powerful Jewish family of the Maccabees managed to free Judah from the Syrians who had by then been controlling it for some time. Eventually they even managed to push the national boundaries outwards until something like the old Davidic kingdom of Israel had been recreated. In the process, Galilee was annexed (104–103 B.C.) and once again became Jewish – and not just in name, for its inhabitants were obliged to be circumcised (the physical sign of Judaism) and to worship Yahweh. The territories around Galilee, however, remained non-Jewish.

The success of the new kingdom was fairly short-lived, for the reigning family was unseated both by internal squabbles and by the Romans, whom it had invited to Jerusalem as a powerful arbitrator to settle those squabbles. Rome installed its own puppet rulers, and itself retained ultimate control of the whole of Palestine. Among these puppet rulers was Herod I, who was styled king. After his death in 4 B.C. his territory was divided among his sons, and one of these, Herod Antipas, took control of Galilee. Though nominally subject to Rome, Antipas actually wielded considerable power.

Galilee, then, had had a chequered history. It had been by turns Jewish, Gentile, and Jewish again; and the general opinion among the pious Jews of Jerusalem was that it was still more Gentile than Jewish. 'Galilee of the Gentiles' they called it, paraphrasing words from the book of Isaiah (Is. 9. 1; cf. Matt. 4. 15). This is not to say that the Jewish religion had no appeal to the Galileans. Many of them wanted to free their land, and indeed the whole of Palestine, from Roman control; so many in fact that the name 'Galilean' became synonymous for 'rebel'. And like all those who in previous centuries had fought for the freedom and supremacy of the Jewish people, they used the Jewish religion as their rallying point. Nevertheless most other Jews regarded the Galileans in general as rough and rather pagan creatures, 'stupid Galileans', and made a great joke of their incomprehensible northern speech. It was the last area from which a great religious teacher was expected to come.

The carpenter

Was Jesus really a carpenter by trade? It seems such an odd thing for anyone to invent that most biblical critics have accepted it as fact, though they point out that some doubt is introduced by Matthew calling him not 'the carpenter' as does Mark (6. 3) but 'the carpenter's son' (Matt. 13. 55). There is also the complication that the word in the original Greek (*tektōn*) may mean a worker not just in wood but also in stone and metal, so that 'craftsman' might be a better translation. Speculations as to the precise nature of Jesus's or his father's work vary a great deal, and while some historians imagine him in a simple joinery shop others prefer to think of him as quite a prosperous builder. But it would probably be wrong to regard him as too middle-class socially, because the implication of the words of the people who heard him preach in the Synagogue at Nazareth – 'Is this not the carpenter?' – seems to be 'How can somebody from a background like his be a great preacher?'; though of course they might merely be saying 'How can he pose as a great preacher when he is just a local man we all know?' (see Mk. 6. 3, Matt. 13. 55; cf. Lk. 4. 22).

There is one very important question about Jesus's upbringing. Was he or was he not a trained rabbi?

'Rabbi' is a Hebrew word meaning literally 'my master' (Hebrew continued to be the 'book language' of Judaism even though Aramaic was used in daily speech). After the time of Jesus 'rabbi' came to be the official title for ordained ministers of the Jewish religion who presided in the synagogues. But in his lifetime and before, it had not acquired this meaning, and was used simply as a title of respect for certain recognised scholars who studied and interpreted the Jewish religious Law. In John's Gospel, Jesus is on one occasion addressed as 'rabbi' by his disciples (1. 38). Is this meant to be an indication that he was a scholar with formal training? Probably not, for John glosses the first use of the word 'rabbi' as meaning 'teacher' and the second as meaning 'my master', so in neither case does he seem to imply that Jesus had a formal rabbinical training. None of the other Gospels uses the term 'rabbi' of Jesus, and indeed Luke, with his story of the twelve-year-old Jesus astonishing the trained doctors of the Law with his remarkable knowledge, seems to imply that he was self-taught (or as Luke would have said, directly inspired by God) rather than formally educated. Moreover a formal rabbinical training would in Jesus's lifetime probably have meant spending some years in Jerusalem sitting at the feet of a great teacher, since Galilee at that period is unlikely to have been able to offer anything comparable. There is no record of any such period spent in Jerusalem by Jesus during his early years. On the other hand there is no explicit denial of it, and persons from the artisan and craftsman classes often did become rabbis. Certainly if Jesus did have a formal training in the Law it would explain his fluency in it, and also perhaps his growing discontent with it as an exclusive way of life. Not that he would have had to be formally educated to gain at least a working knowledge of it, for it was all around him.

The Law and the Prophets

As the son of God-fearing Jews – and despite Galilee's reputation there is no reason to suppose that Jesus's parents were not devout – he would have been taken to the synagogue every Sabbath. For us to regard this as simply 'going to church' in the modern Christian sense would be inadequate, for though there was of course a large spiritual element in the worship of the synagogue it was also a training in Jewish history. This was because the religion of the Jewish people was, and always had been, inextricable from its national history. It was in fact a religion of history.

Yahweh, the God of Israel, was believed to have shown a special concern for the Jewish people since the beginning of time, and the Jews recorded their history in a manner that demonstrated his involvement in it. They told how the first migration of Jews from Mesopotamia to Palestine had been brought about by Yahweh's summons to Abraham to leave the country of his fathers and to journey to the promised land of Canaan (the earlier name for Palestine). They told how at a later period in Jewish history a great number of their people suffered slavery in Egypt, and were released from that slavery and brought back to Palestine through the power of Yahweh and under the leadership of his servant Moses. Most important of all, they recorded how, during this 'exodus' from Egypt, Yahweh had made a 'Covenant' with the Jews, promising that if they would obey his commandments he would make them supreme above all other nations.

It was believed that the fluctuating fortunes of the Jewish settlers in Palestine after their exodus from Egypt were the direct result of Yahweh's intervention, and of their own fidelity or infidelity to their side of the Covenant. Jewish historians explained the brilliant success of David's kingship as the consequence of Yahweh's power, and they attributed the later decline of Jewish fortunes to Israel's disobedience. Moreover they looked to the future, to the day when at last Yahweh would fulfil his Covenant and make Israel supreme above all other nations.

The books of Jewish history in which these events and their interpretations are recorded are found in that part of the Bible known to Christians as the Old Testament. The Jews in the time of Jesus knew it by a different name, 'the Law and the Prophets'. By 'the Law' they meant the five books supposed to have been written by Moses: Genesis, Exodus, Leviticus, Numbers and Deuteronomy. 'The Prophets' was the collective title for the books of Joshua, Judges, Samuel and Kings – actually historical books but supposed to be by prophetic authors – and those of Isaiah, Jeremiah, and other later prophets. 'The Law and the Prophets' were regarded as beyond doubt holy writings in which divinely inspired authors had recorded the word of God. There were also other historical writings, such as the books of Chronicles, Ezra and Daniel, which were highly esteemed but not treated with quite the same awe.

Readings from the Law and the Prophets were prescribed as part of the worship in the synagogue on the Sabbath. Moreover the Law was supposed to govern every detail of a Jew's daily life. 'You shall have no other gods to set against me. You shall not make a carved image for yourself ... You should not make wrong use of the name of the Lord your God. Remember to keep the sabbath day holy ...'. In such words as these, recorded in chapter 20 of the book of Exodus, Yahweh was believed to have delivered his Law to Moses on Mount Sinai after Moses had led the Israelites out of captivity in Egypt. Nor were these commandments regarded simply as moral precepts for the conducting of a right and holy life. They were one side of a crucial bargain, that Yahweh would reward Israel if it kept the Law.

There was much more to the Law than the Ten Commandments from which the words above are quoted. Through the five books of Moses are found explicit instructions as to how the Israelites should carry out the will of Yahweh – or rather the will of 'the Lord', for Yahweh's name was considered to be so sacred that it was rarely used. 'The Lord' was the term most frequently employed, though the word 'God' alone is often found in the Old Testament.

Here are a few of these explicit instructions, which covered all aspects of daily life:

When one man injures and disfigures his fellow-countryman, it shall be done to him as he has done; fracture for fracture, eye for eye, tooth for tooth; the injury and disfigurement that he has inflicted upon another shall in turn be inflicted upon him. (Lev. 24. 19–20)

Of all animals on land these are the creatures you may eat: you may eat any animal which has a parted foot or a cloven hoof and also chews the cud; those which have only a cloven hoof or only chew the cud you may not eat. (Lev. 11. 2–4)

You shall not eat meat with the blood in it. You shall not practise divination or soothsaying. You shall not round off your hair from side to side, and you shall not shave the edge of your beards. (Lev. 19. 26–27)

Many instructions concerned the offering of sacrifice in the temple at Jerusalem:

When any man among you presents an animal as an offering to the Lord . . . he shall slaughter the bull before the Lord, and the Aaronite priests shall present the blood and fling it against the altar all round at the entrance of the Tent of the Presence. He shall then flay the victim and cut it up . . . and the priest shall burn it all on the altar as a whole-offering, a food-offering of soothing odour to the Lord. (Lev. 1. 2, 5–6, 9)

To us, the Law seems harsh. Not only did it command that murderers and even those who killed accidentally should die, but also 'whoever curses his father or his mother shall be put to death' (Ex. 21. 17). To take another example, should a man or woman be gored by an ox which was already known to be a dangerous animal but which had not been properly penned up, then 'the ox shall be stoned, and the owner shall be put to death as well' (Ex. 21. 29). Such was the general tone of the Law.

Despite Jewish belief to the contrary, the Law did not in fact originate *en bloc* in the time of Moses. The handiwork of different generations may be seen in its various layers of composition, of which the earliest probably dates from about 850 B.C. and the latest from about two hundred years later. Moreover later Jewish jurists did make some attempt to liberalise the original more severe laws. The result of this was the book of Deuteronomy or 'Second Law', the text of which dates from the seventh century B.C., though it may incorporate earlier traditions. Yet even this later more liberal version of the Law could scarcely be called humane by modern standards:

When a man has a son who is disobedient and out of control, and will not obey his father or his mother, or pay attention when they punish him, then his father and mother shall take hold of him and bring him out to the elders of the town, at the town gate. They shall say to the elders of the town, 'This son of ours is disobedient and out of control; he will not obey us, he is a wastrel and a drunkard.' Then all the men of the town shall stone him to death, and you will thereby rid yourselves of this wickedness. All Israel will hear of it and be afraid. (Deut. 21. 21)

Such drastic measures were probably not still carried out in the time of Jesus. Nevertheless the Law continued to rule severely over Jewish life.

This written Law of Moses dealt with every aspect of Jewish religious and social life, and it might be thought that it left nothing in doubt. But by the time of Jesus there had been in existence for many generations an even more detailed tradition of oral interpretation of the Law. This had begun for the simple reason that no standard text of the Law originally existed, so that it was not always possible to determine precisely what it laid down. Moreover laws sometimes contradicted each other, and at times their application to particular cases was not clear. This meant that skilled interpreters were needed: hence the coming into existence of 'Scribes' or doctors of the law who had themselves studied the subject thoroughly and could pass their interpretations on to disciples. By the time of Jesus the existence of these Scribes was as much taken for granted as was the Law itself. Moreover the interpretations that they offered had themselves come to be governed severely by precedent and tradition, just as are modern legal judgements. Scribes could no longer interpret freely, but must pass on the teaching of their masters, who in turn had taught what his own master had said. In this way the Scribes' tradition was believed to stretch back to Moses himself. Eventually, some generations after the death of Jesus, this oral interpretative tradition was itself codified and written down in the *Mishnah* ('repetition'), but in his lifetime it still existed only in oral form. This was why young men who were intent on becoming Scribes had to undergo a very severe course of study, listening to their master's words and committing every detail to memory.

We do not know how much of this oral tradition Jesus knew in detail. It is doubtful if, as a Galilean, remote from Jerusalem, he would have been versed in the finer points of legal debate. If there were Scribes resident in his part of Galilee, they would probably have been unsophisticated, provincial men, out of touch with the complex teaching of their Jerusalem counterparts. But certainly the reading aloud of the written Law (in Hebrew, with a translator rendering it into Aramaic) formed the centrepiece of Sabbath worship during Jesus's childhood and early years at Nazareth. Moreover if, as seems likely, he came from a God-fearing family, the whole body of the Law – generally known as the *Torah* or 'teaching' – must have overshadowed his life, much as it did the early years of Paul of Tarsus, who remarked ironically, '... except through law I should never have become acquainted with sin. For example, I should never have known what it was to covet, if the law had not said, "Thou shalt not covet" ' (Rom. 7. 8).

After the reading of the Law in the synagogue would come a reading from the Prophets. Nowadays we are perhaps inclined to think of the ancient Jewish prophets simply in terms of their foretelling of the future, and this was of course one aspect of the prophetic calling. But in the history of Israel they had a very practical function: they summoned men back to the worship of Yahweh, and in doing so they strengthened the national resolve and hope for the future. Their role was thus in a sense as much political as it was religious. No better example of this can be found than the anonymous prophet usually known as Second Isaiah, so called because though he composed much of the later part of the book of Isaiah his real name is unknown. He was among the exiles from Jerusalem living in captivity in Babylon during the sixth century B.C., and in the midst of their general despair he promised them a glorious future:

> Comfort, comfort my people; – it is the voice of your God; speak tenderly to Jerusalem and tell her this, that she has fulfilled her term of bondage, that her penalty is paid ... Every valley shall be lifted up, every mountain and hill brought down ... Here is the Lord God coming in might, coming to rule with his right arm. (Is. 40. 1–2, 4, 10)

Second Isaiah's rallying call to Israel and his vindication of the supreme power of its God undoubtedly had a powerful effect on the nation, and helped to rebuild its confidence after exile. Similarly in earlier centuries a long line of other prophets – Jeremiah, Elijah, Samuel, Moses himself – had in their turn guided the fortunes of Israel. But as it happened Second Isaiah was almost the last of the prophets.

After him a few prophetic voices such as Haggai, Zechariah

and Malachi still spoke, but they were not of his stature, and with the Israelites' return from captivity towards the end of the sixth century B.C. the prophetic tradition virtually died out. Certainly writings of a prophetic character still emerged, but these were now presented as if they were the work of an earlier age. For example the book of Daniel purports to have been written during the Babylonian exile, whereas in fact it dates from about four hundred years later, and is really a thinly veiled allegory of the troubles that Jerusalem was going through at the time; Nebuchadnezzar the king of Babylon stands for the Syrian tyrant Antiochus IV who was trying to suppress Jewish religion. Fine as such writings are – and 'Daniel' contributed greatly to the development of later Jewish thought – they do not have the character of the old prophets.

Why had prophecy ceased? The answer is easily found. The Law had really taken its place. In the earlier history of Israel the Law had not really been a law at all but merely a record of current practice. The business of pushing forward the spiritual and ethical frontiers had been left largely to the prophets and their followers – for there were 'schools' of prophecy, and some prophetic books represent the work of a number of people, sometimes spanning many generations. But later the intellectual energy of Judaism had largely been taken over by the Scribes, who studied and interpreted the Law; and they directed this energy towards legal interpretation rather than prophetic utterance. As a result Judaism had become largely a religion of the Law. Meanwhile the disappearance of the prophetic element was greatly regretted. A historian writing in the second century B.C. describes the misery that was then afflicting Israel by saying that it was 'worse than any since the day when prophets ceased to appear' (Macc. 9. 27).

Jesus, then, would have heard the Law and the Prophets read in the synagogue each Sabbath, and it would be a dull young man who would not find excitement in the writings of the Prophets. He too must have regretted, as so many did, the disappearance of prophecy. And he could hardly fail to be gripped by the news, which came one day when he was in his late twenties, that a new prophet had suddenly appeared on the bank of the river Jordan, crying, 'Repent, for the kingdom of God is at hand!'

3 The kingdom of God

The kingdom of God

The Gospel writers found this new prophet, John the Baptist, such an awkward fact that they can scarcely have invented him. He did not fit into their pattern, and though they tried to imply that he was some kind of reincarnation of Elijah, whose reappearance in Israel was expected by the Jews as a portent of the coming of the Messiah, John the Baptist himself denies this in John's Gospel:

> . . . the Jews of Jerusalem sent a deputation of priests and Levites to ask him who he was . . . 'Are you Elijah?' 'No' he replied. (Jn. 1. 19, 21)

As to the notion of Jesus, the sinless Messiah, being baptised by John as a sign that he had repented of his sins and been forgiven, Matthew finds this so uncomfortable that he has Jesus explaining to John the Baptist that it is really only being done 'to conform . . . with all that God requires', which presumably means for show rather than through necessity (Matt. 3. 15). All this leads one to suppose that Jesus's baptism by John is a sound historical fact.

Jesus had already been physically initiated into the Jewish religion by circumcision, which was performed on all male children when they were eight days old. A rite such as baptism would therefore seem to many Jews to be unnecessary. But ritual washings-away of spiritual uncleanness are found in a number of religions, and in Jesus's day something resembling John's baptism was actually practised, along with circumcision, by Gentiles who became Jewish converts. So baptism would certainly not have been a new idea to Jesus. On the other hand the special emphasis John gave to it was obviously thought to be unusual; hence his title 'the Baptist'.

Not long after his Baptism and at about the age of thirty, Jesus began to go about in Galilee preaching the message he had heard John announce: 'The kingdom of God is at hand.' What exactly did this message mean?

A hope for the future

We have already seen that Judaism was a religion of history. It looked back on what God had done for Israel and declared that his deeds in former days proved his power. But it did not content itself with merely looking at the past. How could it, when the great promise of God's Covenant had yet to be fulfilled? On Mount Sinai after Moses had led the Israelites out of Egypt, God promised them that 'out of all peoples you shall become my special possession' (Ex. 19. 5), and this promise had been renewed time and again through the voices of God's prophets. Moreover, at such great moments in its history as the victorious kingship of David and the release from Babylonian captivity, Israel thought it had seen a very real demonstration that God was keeping this Covenant. Admittedly it had not been completely kept; God had not yet utterly fulfilled his promise. However, there was no question but that he would do so. All that was holding him back was the recalcitrance of Israel itself, its refusal to obey his voice and keep his Law. When true repentance was achieved by Israel and the nation at last managed to keep its own side of the Covenant, then would come the time of glory.

But Israel did repent, or at least many of its people did so, very often, and the time of glory did not come. While it was impossible to say that Israel had ever reached a state of complete sinlessness, there were nevertheless many holy men numbered among it. Moreover, however numerous Israel's sins, she had certainly suffered for them, suffered so much that forgiveness and the coming of the glorious time was surely due. And this was exactly what Second Isaiah said was going to happen; in captivity at Babylon he told the Israelites that God declared their nation's sins forgiven: 'she has fulfilled her term of bondage . . . she has received at the Lord's hand double measure for all her sin' (Is. 40. 2). And now, he declared, she would at last be raised above all nations:

> Now shall all who defy you be disappointed and put to shame; all who set themselves against you shall be as nothing; they shall vanish. You will look for your assailants but not find them; all who take up arms against you shall be as nothing, nothing at all. For I, the Lord your God, take you by the right hand . . . (Is. 41. 11–13)

Yet in the event this was not what happened. Certainly Israel was released from captivity, and the nation to some extent rebuilt itself; but there was no triumph such as Second Isaiah had promised, and instead a succession of foreign powers interfered with the internal government of the country.

It is conceivable that in the face of this continual frustration of hope, Israel might have abandoned the worship of Yahweh. But it did not. Instead it began to believe that its triumph over other nations would come about not through the natural course of worldly events, but through some kind of supernatural intervention by the deity. The idea grew up, in fact, that Yahweh would fulfil his Covenant not simply by making Israel supreme above nations, but by bringing about the actual end of the world through some kind of cosmic catastrophe. Then would come a great Judgement, in which Yahweh himself would condemn sinners to destruction and would reward the righteous – by which was meant the righteous Israelites. These Israelites would then, at last, be made supreme above all nations. As God's 'saints' they would command the whole earth, or the new earth that had been fashioned. All other peoples would obey them.

This was the sort of thing that many people in Israel came to expect. Not that everyone agreed on the precise details of what would happen. The picture varied greatly from sect to sect. Meanwhile there were always those who refused to allow their hope of Israel's coming triumph to be made so exclusively supernatural, and who continued to expect that in the present world-order a new king David would arrive and lead Israel to victory. There were also a number of people in Israel who had no interest in such things at all, and who regarded them as newfangled fanciful beliefs which were adulterating the worship of Yahweh and the keeping of his Law.

The ways of referring to the expected intervention by Yahweh varied, but more and more it came to be expressed in terms of Yahweh's 'kingdom'. Israel had always associated its God with kingship, and it was quite natural for it to describe the idea of him intervening directly in the physical world as his appearing in kingly might. Second Isaiah had this in mind when he wrote: 'Here is the Lord God coming in might, coming to rule with his right arm.' (Is. 40. 10)

God's kingly rule and the end of the world which many people believed would usher it in formed the subject of numerous 'apocalyptic' or visionary writings in the centuries before the birth of Jesus. Few of these were thought to have sufficient authority to be added to the canon of Jewish holy writ, but one that did pass the test was the book of Daniel, in the seventh chapter of which is a vision (couched in symbolical terms) of the events which it was believed would lead to the coming of God's 'kingdom'. Daniel sees four huge beasts ravaging the world (the four contemporary world powers), and, as he watches, these beasts are killed or subdued by 'one ancient in years', that is, God himself. Then he sees 'one like a son of man coming with the clouds of heaven', and this 'son of man' (a Jewish tautology for 'man') is given kingly power over the earth, so that all nations serve him. When Daniel asks for an interpretation of this vision he is told that the 'son of man' stands for the righteous Israelites, who will be given sovereignty over the earth.

It will be noted that there is one peculiar feature here, the 'son of man' whose coming 'with the clouds of heaven' ushers in God's kingly rule. We shall need to look at this very carefully later, for it is crucial to the question of Jesus's own role. But for the moment it is enough to note the general features of the Daniel passage: the warring nations which are subdued through the direct intervention of God, and the coming of a 'kingly power' through which God's people in Israel will rule over the whole earth. This was the sort of expectation which existed in Jesus's time. What we do not know is whether most people believed that the kingdom of God (or 'kingdom of heaven', a phrase often used as an alternative) would come soon. Probably this varied from person to person. No doubt many people thought that, while the kingdom of God was something that would certainly arrive one day, only a foolish man would predict that its coming was certainly very near. On the other hand there must have been fanatics, just as there are on street corners today, who made a loud parade of their belief that the long awaited event was about to happen – 'The end of the world is at hand!'

By this criterion, John the Baptist and Jesus were fanatics.

What did Jesus believe?

Or were they? Not surprisingly, many Christian theologians are uncomfortable about the notion that Jesus went about preaching that God was shortly – very shortly – going to intervene dramatically in the history of the world, in a literally earth-shattering event that would usher in a new age. For of course this did not happen. Both in Jesus's lifetime and afterwards, the world went on very much as it had before. And the idea that Jesus was wrong disconcerts many Christians – though there are some who say that he spoke in the phraseology of his time, and was limited by the contemporary intellectual outlook, which does not (they say) in any way devalue his importance for modern believers.

It is of course perfectly possible to read the Gospels without realising that Jesus was preaching a message about the nearness of the end of the world. Though that phrase 'the kingdom of

God' is central to his teaching, and though there are certainly (as we shall see) a number of passages where he specifically refers to the coming crisis, these things do not dominate the Gospels to the exclusion of all else. The reader's attention can easily be drawn away from them to the parables (though these are in fact largely about 'the kingdom'), to the healings and other miracles, and of course to the trial, death and resurrection of Jesus. Moreover the Church from the time of Paul onwards has realised the danger of over-emphasising the 'end of the world' element of Jesus's message, and has drawn attention away from it and focused much more on the importance of Jesus himself. Not until the nineteenth century, when scholars re-examined the Bible in a more candid way than was previously possible, did the realisation dawn that at the centre of Jesus's teaching was this alarming set of notions about a cosmic calamity and the physical coming of the kingdom. Albert Schweitzer's *Quest of the Historical Jesus* (1906) is in fact not just a survey of nineteenth-century writings about Jesus but also an eloquent, though rather exaggerated, plea that we should at last come face to face with the fact that the imminent coming of the kingdom really was what Jesus believed in – in other words that he based his life's work on a mistake.

Naturally the writings of Schweitzer and others who held the same view produced a reaction, one result of which was the work of the English biblical scholar C. H. Dodd. Writing in the 1930s, Dodd put forward the view that while Jesus was certainly talking about the kingdom of God he did not believe that it was about to come, but that *it had begun to arrive already.* Jesus felt (Dodd suggested) that, far from being a merely future event, the kingdom was being made visible on earth in his own work as a healer and preacher. Far from being mistaken, Jesus saw the truth about himself and his role.

Dodd had no great difficulty in making this interpretation seem plausible. He suggested that the words 'the kingdom of God is at hand' (found in the English translations of the Bible up to that time) were a wrong rendering of the original Greek, and that 'the kingdom of God is *upon* you', that is, already arriving, would be better. The New English Bible of which Dodd was a principal translator adopts this rendering (see Mk. 1. 15, Matt. 3. 2, 4. 17). As to the various predictions that Jesus is said to have made of cosmic events which would usher in the kingdom, Dodd regarded these as later interpolations by people who could not help thinking conventionally in terms of a strictly future coming of the kingdom, rather than the 'realised' kingdom which Jesus preached.

Dodd's views require a great deal of selection and re-interpretation of material in the Gospels, and, chiefly for this reason, they have not been widely accepted. So: are we left once again with a Jesus whose expectations were quite plainly of an imminent end of the world, a Jesus who in fact was wrong? And, if so, how crucial was his mistake? Did his message depend entirely on his belief that the end was near, and is it negated by our knowledge that he was mistaken? We shall begin to see the answer when we have examined in some detail the character of his teaching.

4 The Law is not enough

The Gospels are so full of the sayings of Jesus that it ought to be possible to recover the precise nature of his teaching. In fact it is difficult to do so, because of a large number of inconsistencies and even contradictions.

To take one example of this, in Mark 10. 9 Jesus forbids divorce unconditionally, with the words: 'What God has joined together, man must not separate.' On the other hand Matthew's version of this saying makes Jesus add a saving clause: 'if a man divorces his wife *for any cause other than unchastity*, and marries another, he commits adultery' (Matt. 19. 9). Clearly this alters the whole position.

This kind of confusion often occurs when the attempt is made to recover the details of Jesus's teaching, and nobody can agree on a criterion for resolving it. Are we to accept as authentic only those sayings which reflect Jesus's Jewish background and his debt to the Law, or only those which show his individuality? Associated with this difficulty is the fact that the early Church simply did not take the trouble to record Jesus's teachings as often as one might expect. Paul, for instance, in all his Letters scarcely ever tells his readers what the earthly Jesus specifically taught about something.

In the face of this it is understandable that many historians have despaired of recovering Jesus's teaching. Indeed it is probably foolish to try to reconstruct it in precise detail. On the other hand we cannot really pretend that the problems of the text obscure the character of that teaching, a character which becomes all the more plain when one compares Jesus – as I shall now do – with other Jewish teachers of his time.

Hillel and Shammai

If one is looking for religious teachers in first century Judaism with whom to compare Jesus, two figures stand out. They were both Scribes, that is, their life's work was a study of the Law and its interpretation; and they were both members of the religious group within Judaism known as the 'Pharisees', a name which probably means 'separated ones'. But despite these similarities between the two men, their teaching differed radically.

Hillel came from a poor background and had travelled from

the Babylonian 'Dispersion' (Jews living outside Israel) to Jerusalem, where he worked as a labourer in order to keep himself while studying the Law. Eventually he became the leader of a scribal school which, like the others of its kind, was characterised by its intense discussions on legal issues. Hillel's discussions and those of his disciples were usually carried on with a school of opposing views, led by the severely conservative rabbi Shammai. Hillel was a moral optimist with a faith in humanity and divine justice; he felt that the Law should be an instrument of life-giving rather than of deadly rectitude, and he gave judgements with 'the greater good' in mind, rather than basing his decisions on the niceties of legal interpretation. He was an example of the liberal and reforming element which has always been present within Judaism. In contrast, Shammai typified the Jew who observed the Law scrupulously, with much attention to detailed precepts. He was the kind of Pharisee who believed that God himself studied the Law daily. It was said of him that once at the Feast of Tabernacles, a time when all male Jews were required by the Law to sit within a tabernacle or tent to remind them of their tent-dwelling nomadic days, his daughter-in-law gave birth to a boy. Shammai broke open the roof over the bed where she and the child lay, and built a special booth, so that his grandson might keep the Law and sit (or at least lie) within the tabernacle.

It is revealing to set the teachings of these two men alongside those of Jesus. Like Jesus, they wrote no books, and the record of what they had said was for many years carried solely in the memories of their disciples. Not until the second century were their sayings written in the *Mishnah.*

The comparison is best made topic by topic, choosing crucial areas of Jewish life about which all three men had something to say.

Marriage, adultery and divorce

The Jews regarded marriage as pre-eminently a means by which a man might produce heirs. Monogamy was not considered an overwhelmingly binding principle, and it was told of Abraham that because his wife was barren he had a child by a slave woman. Wives could be divorced simply on the ground of their infertility; no other reason was necessary for the dissolution of the marriage. Similarly the Scribes considered that the Law's injunction to 'Be fruitful and increase' (Gen. I. 22) was a command to a married couple that they must have children. The only difference of opinion was over how many children must be born before abstention from further procreation could be allowed. Shammai said a man must have two sons before he and his wife abstained; the more liberal Hillel, who apparently had a higher regard for daughters, said that one son and one daughter was enough.

As to adultery, the written Law was perfectly clear in its command:

When a man is discovered lying with a married woman, they shall both die, the woman as well as the man who lay with her: you shall rid Israel of this wickedness. (Deut. 22. 22)

In fact by the time of Shammai, Hillel and Jesus the death penalty was no longer imposed on persons found guilty of adultery, but the slightest suspicion of unfaithfulness in a wife was enough to expose her to the public shame. Moreover it was taken for granted that in such circumstances the husband would divorce her. The only question was whether the wording of the Law allowed him to divorce her on any other grounds.

What the written Law actually allowed was that when a man had married a wife, if she 'does not win his favour because he finds something shameful in her', then he could write her a note of divorce (Deut. 24. 1). Shammai said that this referred solely to indecency, and that no other cause for divorce could be allowed. Hillel, however, was more liberal in his attitude to the Law – that is, he interpreted it more freely, though the net result was certainly not liberal in the ethical sense. He declared that the wording of the Law meant a husband could divorce his wife merely because small details of her conduct displeased him – even if she just 'spoiled a dish for him'. Moreover a third scribe, Rabbi Akiba, thought that the Law's words 'she does not win his favour' meant that the husband could divorce the wife simply because he had found another woman whom he preferred.

Against the background of these views, the ambiguity in the Gospel records of Jesus's teaching on divorce becomes comparatively insignficant, and the character of his views stands out clearly. Here is Matthew's version of what he is reported to have said:

Some Pharisees came and tested him by asking, 'Is it lawful for a man to divorce his wife on any and every ground?' He asked in return, 'Have you never read that the Creator made them from the beginning male and female?'; and he added, 'For this reason a man shall leave his father and mother, and be made one with his wife; and the two shall become one flesh. It follows that they are no longer two individuals: they are one flesh. What God has joined together, man must not separate.' 'Why then', they objected, 'did Moses lay it down that a man might divorce his wife by note of dismissal?' He answered, 'It was because your minds were closed that Moses gave you permission to divorce your wives; but it was not like that when all began. I tell you, if a man divorces his wife for any cause other than unchastity, and marries another, he commits adultery.' (Matt. 19. 3–9)

Jesus's method of argument here resembles that of the Scribes. He takes a verse from the written Law as the basis of his judgement: 'male and female he created them' (Gen. 1. 27). To this he adds a second text: 'That is why a man leaves his father and mother and is united to his wife, and the two become one flesh' (Gen. 2. 24). This, he concludes, proves that God wishes marriage to be indissoluble. He even displays something of the subtlety – one could almost say wiliness – of rabbinical exegesis, for the first words of the second text ('That is why man . . .') do not in their original context refer to the first text at all, but to the creation of Eve out of Adam's rib. But then suddenly he departs radically from the Scribes' methods. When his questioners ask him why the conclusion he has reached is in contradiction to the written Law of Moses – they are thinking of the text in Deuteronomy that permits divorce – he does not reply by asserting his case through further scriptural exegesis, as a Scribe would have done, but by saying in effect: 'Moses had to compromise, because he knew you could not keep the ultimate commandment that God had given you.'

If this passage is an authentic record of Jesus's teaching, his approach was radical in the extreme. He is telling the Pharisees that the Law of Moses, which they (and indeed the whole of Judaism) regard as the rule by which everything is governed, is in fact no more than a compromise, the work of a man who knew that God demanded something more. Moreover Jesus reaches this conclusion by confronting the fact that texts from the Law can contradict one another – an extraordinarily daring thing to do, for it was assumed by Jews that the Law could not possibly contradict itself.

Nor is this Jesus's only departure, in this passage, from the Scribal approach. The questioners have set him a problem typical of those which exercised the rabbinical schools, the very question in fact over which Hillel and Shammai debated. They want to know how he interprets the controversial Deuteronomy clause permitting divorce. What precisely does he regard as the grounds on which divorce may be allowed? Jesus responds by not answering the question at all. He tells them that their whole approach is morally completely wrong, that this clause – and by implication others of its kind – is one of the compromises that the Law has regrettably had to make 'because your minds were closed'. Such compromises are not for one moment the *total* will of God. And in the face of all their negative legislation with its prohibitions and conditions and limitations he throws this clear doctrine of marriage: 'What God has joined together, man must not separate.'

After this, it is certainly surprising to find him admitting a saving clause 'for any cause other than unchastity' into his own doctrine. He may of course be simply reflecting current Jewish practice; in other words, divorce on the grounds of adultery may have been regarded as inevitable even by him. Or perhaps the implication is that when a married person commits adultery the marriage has already been destroyed. On the other hand it may be that Matthew, or the earlier oral Christian tradition, has inserted the words 'for any cause other than unchastity' into Jesus's pronouncement so as to make it a particular ruling for the Church, which had perhaps found it impossible to forbid divorce when adultery had taken place. We do not know what the truth is, and for this reason it is most unwise, here and elsewhere, to use Jesus's word as a new Law to govern precise details of behaviour. What matters is the manner in which he approaches the issue, a manner that was startlingly different from that of legalistic Judaism.

Poverty and wealth

In Mark's Gospel, Jesus is recorded as saying to a rich man: 'sell everything you have, and give to the poor' (Mk. 10. 21). Commentators have pointed out that if this is taken as a literal commandment for everyone it is impractical and unrealistic. Even monastic communities which embrace poverty retain some kind of financial resources with which to make their way of life possible, while for the Christian living in the world and earning his keep this injunction, if taken literally, is clearly absurd. Generosity to the poor may be of paramount importance, but how can people sell *all* that they have? This, at any rate, is how some have responded to these words. But if we want to see why Jesus said them (or is reported to have said them) we need only look at the teachings of his contemporaries to discover what prompted him.

Judaism believed that poverty was pleasing to God, and it included among its number at least one sect, the Essenes, whose members held all property communally and lived somewhat in the manner of poor people. On the other hand riches were regarded as the reward of righteousness. Many Jews led a life of some affluence, especially as farmers, vineyard owners, and cultivators of olive trees, the latter particularly in Galilee where olive oil was a major export. To such as these the Law gave a general injunction:

The poor will always be with you in the land, and for that reason I [Moses] command you to be open-handed with your countrymen, both poor and distressed . . . (Deut. 15. 11)

But what did this mean in specific terms? Over the generations the Scribes established detailed rules for assisting those in need; for example:

A poor man that is journeying from place to place should be given not less than one loaf . . . If he spends the night he should be given what is needful to support him for the night. If he stays over the Sabbath he should be given enough food for three meals. If a man has food enough for two meals he may not take anything from the Paupers' Dish, and if enough for fourteen meals he may not take anything from the Poor-Fund.

Provision was made against starvation, but care was also taken that the poor should not be given more than they needed.

Alongside a system for the relief of poverty in general, Judaism also had strict rules about *peah* or 'gleanings'. This meant that a certain part of crops and of the produce of vineyards and olive groves was set aside for the poor to help themselves. It was definitely implied both in written Law and the oral tradition that when the harvest was abundant or poverty was especially severe, *peah* should be given generously. On the other hand the Scribes also said that 'it should not be less than one sixtieth part' of the harvest, and the nature of the disputes which arose over *peah* suggests that the average farmer was not over-keen to exceed this stipulated minimum, which of course only made a very small demand on him. When plots of grain were sown between olive trees, was it necessary (asked the Scribes) to grant *peah* from each plot individually or just from one to serve for all? Shammai's school said that the sixtieth portion must be taken from each of the plots, a very finicky procedure for the farmer, though arguably the fairest way. Hillel's pupils thought it was enough to calculate what was due on all the plots together, and then to take this amount out of one plot, which would be much easier. This sort of dispute characterised the Jewish poor laws and the people who interpreted them. Against this background, Jesus's attitude to the question of poverty and wealth is a shock:

As he was starting out on a journey, a stranger ran up, and, kneeling before him, asked, 'Good Master, what must I do to win eternal life?' Jesus said to him, 'Why do you call me good? No one is good except God alone. You know the commandments: "Do not murder; do not commit adultery; do not steal; do not give false evidence; do not defraud; honour your father and mother." ' 'But, Master,' he replied, 'I have kept all these since I was a boy.' Jesus looked straight at him; his heart warmed to him, and he said, 'One thing you lack: go, sell everything you have, and give to the poor, and you will have riches in heaven; and come, follow me.' At these words his face fell and he went away with a heavy heart; for he was a man of great wealth. (Mk. 10. 17–22; cf. Matt. 19. 16–22. Lk. 18. 18–23)

To the question 'what must I do to win eternal life?' Jesus first gives the conventional Jewish answer, 'You must keep the Law'; for the commandments he quotes are those six of the Ten Commandments which deal with ethics. But his questioner is not satisfied. He has kept the Law, yet finds that something is still lacking. In answer to this, Jesus says in effect: 'Yes, you are right. God *does* command you to do more than keep the Law which you have known from childhood. You, a rich man, should sell everything that you have and give the money to the poor.'

Compared to the attitude taken by the Scribes, this is remarkable. But we have to ask: is it meant to be a general rule to be kept by all, or is it merely an answer to this particular wealthy man? We really cannot be certain. On the one hand Jesus is not reported to have enjoined compulsory poverty on all his followers. On the other hand the general tone of his ministry seems to have been one of compassion for the poor and outcast rather than for the rich, and indeed Mark's narrative continues (after this episode) with Jesus telling his disciples, 'It is easier for a camel to pass through the eye of a needle than for a rich man to enter the kingdom of God' (Mk 10. 25) – a saying which the medieval church found so hard to accept that it invented a totally fictitious gate at Jerusalem called the Needle's Eye, so as to soften the impact of Jesus's words.

What we can say for certain is first that Jesus tells the man *to keep the Law*—we must not miss this—and then he says that keeping the Law *is not enough.*

The seventh day

The Law ordered the Jews to keep one day in every seven as a holy Sabbath, on which no work was to be done. By the time of Jesus the observance of this Sabbath was governed by minutely detailed rules, developed by the oral tradition of the Law, which delineated precisely what constituted work and what did not. For example:

> The School of Shammai say: Ink, dyestuffs, or vetches may not be soaked [on the day before the Sabbath] unless there is time for them to be wholly soaked the same day. And the School of Hillel permit it. The School of Shammai say: Bundles of flax may not be put in an oven unless there is time for them to steam off the same day. And the School of Hillel permit it.

And here is a rule, one of many, about which there was no dispute, which delineates precisely what kind of 'work' profaned the Sabbath:

> If a poor man stood outside and the householder inside, and the poor man stretched his hand inside and put aught into the householder's hand, or took anything from it and brought it out, the poor man is culpable and the householder is not culpable. If the householder stretched his hand outside and put anything into the poor man's hand, or took anything from it and brought it in, the householder is culpable and the poor man is not culpable. But if the poor man stretched his hand inside and the householder took anything from it, or put anything into it and the poor man brought it out, neither is culpable; and if the householder stretched his hand outside and the poor man took anything from it, or put anything into it and the householder brought it in, neither is culpable.

There are more than a hundred such clauses in the *Mishnah*, and they show that the Sabbath was regarded as a self-justifying institution, something to be observed for its own sake, without asking in what way God's will was being served by doing so. The Law ordained that the Sabbath should be observed, and that was enough. There was to be no questioning, no consideration of priorities.

We need to fix this firmly in our minds before we turn to the question of Jesus's attitude to the Sabbath, because the evidence appears at first sight to be contradictory. On some occasions he appears to be taking the prohibition of work on the Sabbath seriously. He does not heal a large crowd of sick people until 'after sunset' on the Sabbath, that is, the hour at which the prohibition was lifted (Mk 1. 32). Moreover he himself is recorded as attending the synagogue and preaching on the Sabbath (Mk 1. 21; cf Lk 4. 16 ff). Yet at other times he seems to be attacking the whole Sabbath concept. Mark and the other Synoptics record how he heals a man with a withered hand in the synagogue on the Sabbath (Mk. 3. 1–6, Matt. 12. 9–14, Lk. 6. 6–11). The Scribes and other members of the Pharisaic party regard this as 'work' and thus as forbidden on the Sabbath. In Mark's version, Jesus justifies his actions by asking them rhetorically: 'Is it permitted to do good or to do evil on the Sabbath, to save life or to kill?' At first sight this may seem a slightly obtuse approach to the issue, and it may have puzzled Matthew, for his Gospel records Jesus as saying something rather different:

Suppose you had one sheep, which fell into a ditch on the Sabbath; is there one of you who would not catch hold of it and lift it out? And surely a man is worth far more than a sheep! It is therefore permitted to do good on the Sabbath. (Matt. 12. 11–12)

There is a similar confusion in the story of Jesus and his disciples plucking ears of corn on the Sabbath, which the Pharisees regarded as 'reaping' and therefore forbidden:

One Sabbath he was going through the cornfields; and his disciples, as they went, began to pluck ears of corn. The Pharisees said to him, 'Look, why are they doing what is forbidden on the Sabbath?' He answered, 'Have you never read what David did when he and his men were hungry and had nothing to eat? He went into the House of God, in the time of Abiathar the High Priest, and ate the sacred bread, though no one but a priest is allowed to eat it, and even gave it to his men.'

He also said to them, 'The Sabbath was made for the sake of man and not man for the Sabbath: therefore the Son of Man is sovereign even over the Sabbath.' (Mk. 2. 23–38; cf. Lk. 6. 1–5)

We should note that Jesus justifies his actions first by an allusion to scripture (the episode of David and his men in the 'House of God'), which was the Scribal method; then by the general precept ('The Sabbath was made for the sake of man ...'); and finally by a statement deduced from this precept, that 'the Son of Man' (himself) had power even over the Sabbath. His response to the Scribes is therefore a blend of their own method, of a precept made on his own authority, and of a statement about the nature of that authority.

This is Mark's version of the incident, and Mathew apparently regards it as inadequate, for (unlike Luke, who repeats it virtually verbatim) his Gospel adds another Scribal-style justification to Jesus's words:

Or have you not read in the Law that on the Sabbath the priests in the temple break the Sabbath and it is not held against them? I tell you, there is something greater than the temple here. If you had known what the text means, 'I require mercy, not sacrifice', you would not have condemned the innocent. For the Son of Man is sovereign over the Sabbath. (Matt. 12. 5–8)

The precept about the Sabbath being made for man is entirely absent here – perhaps because Matthew has found it too shocking – and the whole issue is becoming cluttered with yet more allusions to scripture. Paraphrased, Matthew's version reads: 'The Law says that priests in the temple must work on the Sabbath (to offer sacrifices and carry out their other duties) and nobody condemns them for doing it. And here, in myself, is something greater than the temple, so if the temple can override the Sabbath law, so can I even more.' Jesus then quotes a text from Hosea (6. 6) whose meaning here appears to be: 'It is better to be humane about such things than to stick to the letter of the Law.' Finally Matthew picks up Mark's dictum about the Son of Man being lord over the Sabbath.

This is all very confused and confusing, and not surprisingly many commentators doubt whether Jesus is really being very radical. He is after all using all the paraphernalia of rabbinical Judaism to justify his action. Can he be offering any serious criticism of the Law?

Quite possibly he is not. He may simply be proving by rabbinical exegesis that the Law does permit certain exceptions to the Sabbath rule, though precisely what exceptions is not clear. Or he may be declaring that as Son of Man he is 'sovereign over the Sabbath'. Many commentators have decided that this is so, and one theologian even suggests that the precept should read: 'The Sabbath was made for the Son of Man.' If this latter interpretation is accepted then we are left with a Jesus whose prime concern is to prove that he himself is too great a figure to need to keep the Sabbath rule. Now, this may be exactly what he said. (This is not the place to discuss the vital question of whether he thought he was Messiah or Son of Man; the next chapter will tackle that issue.) If on the other hand we are prepared to give some weight to the precept 'The Sabbath was made for the sake of man . . .' Jesus certainly seems to be being radical towards the Law. And if we then turn back to the earlier incident of his healing the man in the synagogue, we seem to find confirmation that in some circumstances at least Jesus is prepared to set the Sabbath rule on one side.

But in what circumstances? It is no good pretending that these two incidents – the healing of the man and the plucking of the ears of corn – add up to anything like a rule of behaviour. Certainly in both cases some element of human discomfort is involved: the man suffers from his withered hand, the disciples are presumably hungry. But to a modern judgement there seems to be far more moral urgency in the former case than in the latter, and we are left totally puzzled and unable to understand what Jesus is aiming to teach about Sabbath observance.

Of course, modern judgement should not be our criterion. It may be that to the first-century Palestinian mind the two cases could be equated morally. It is also possible that the second incident – the plucking of the ears of corn – had no great significance to Jesus himself, and has been recorded simply because it happened to be the occasion of a dispute with his opponents. We should perhaps be wary of putting too much weight on it.

What, then, can we conclude? Certainly that Jesus was known to have broken the Sabbath law on some occasions, and probably that he did so in order to alleviate suffering. Did he have any consistent attitude to the Sabbath? Very possibly not. We must not let too much hang on the precept that the Sabbath was made for man, partly because it was apparently not original to Jesus – Rabbi Simeon ben Menasya is recorded to have said 'The Sabbath is delivered unto you, and you are not delivered to the Sabbath' – and partly because to the modern mind it may suggest the sort of 'humanistic' attitude that was quite foreign to the Jewish mind. We, with our modern moral outlook, may imagine that Jesus was saying: 'The Sabbath was made for man to use as he thinks fit, and man was not made to be the slave of the Sabbath.' No Jew could have said this. The Sabbath had been ordained by God, and to keep the Sabbath was to work his will. There was never any question of *man* being served, either by the keeping of the Sabbath or by an observance of any other precept. The only question which a Jew could legitimately ask was: could it be that sometimes God's will might be obeyed *more fully*, more completely, by setting the Sabbath rule on one side and fulfilling some other command? Might there, in other words, be certain occasions when keeping the established Law was *not enough*?

This, we can now see, is what Jesus is teaching. The healing of the man with the withered arm exemplifies precisely this. The Law may forbid all work on the Sabbath, but that is not the sum of God's will. If Jesus, a healer, is faced with a man who requires his ministrations, then he will heal him then and there, because God regards this as more important than the keeping of the

Sabbath. Not to heal the man would be as wrong as to leave a sheep in a ditch just because it was the Sabbath – something (it seems) that no farmer, however strict a Jew, would do. When Jesus says 'Is it permitted to do good or to do evil on the Sabbath?' he means: 'You can see that God wills me to heal this man. To ignore God's will would be evil.'

This is not to say that Jesus formulates a rule of Sabbath behaviour, or that his attitude to the Sabbath rule is necessarily consistent. Indeed, it *cannot* be consistent. The whole point of his teaching on this issue (and others) is that fixed rules do not work. By simply obeying the Law you cannot be certain that you are carrying out God's commands to the full. Observing the Law may be good, but it is not enough. The issue must be judged and God's will must be listened to in each particular case.

What is uncleanness?

We now come to a passage which has puzzled many commentators. This is the episode where Jesus comments on the Pharisees' observance of the laws of ritual purity.

The incident as narrated by Mark (7. 1–23) runs as follows. The Pharisees remark that Jesus's disciples often eat with unwashed hands, and do not observe the rules about purifying dishes and cups in the manner prescribed by the oral tradition of the Law. They ask Jesus why this is so, and he replies that these rules of purification are merely 'the precepts of men' and not the commandments of God. From this he goes on to condemn a way in which the oral tradition has actually superseded the written Law. He says that there are men (presumably Pharisees) who, rather than support their ageing parents, give their money to the service of the temple. This he says is disobedience to the commandment to 'honour your father and your mother'. Then – and this may well be on another occasion – he declares that the elaborate food laws of Judaism which prescibe what may and may not be eaten are based on a misapprehension:

> . . . nothing that goes into a man from outside can defile him; no, it is the things that come out of him that defile a man . . . For from inside, out of a man's heart, come evil thoughts, acts of fornication, of theft, murder, adultery, ruthless greed, and malice; fraud, indecency, envy, slander, arrogance, and folly; these evil things all come from inside, and they defile the man.

Mark comments: 'Thus he declared all foods clean.'

Did he? If so, he was, as many commentators have observed,

nullifying not just the oral tradition but even the written Law itself, which is very specific about what may be eaten and what may not. There is thus thought to be a contradiction between this and Jesus's remarks earlier in the same passage, where he condemns the Pharisees for *ignoring* the written Law by having too high a regard for the oral tradition. All this has led commentators to suppose that Jesus's criticisms of Judaism were occasional and specific rather than general.

But this is surely missing the point. It is not that Jesus is discussing the relative importance of the written Law and the oral tradition. What he is talking about is – once again – the necessity for realising that the mere keeping of the Law is not enough. People are, he says, failing to observe God's real will. For example they neglect the responsibility of looking after parents in order to be sanctimonious and give their money to the temple. Then again, men scrupulously observe food laws and make sure that nothing 'unclean' goes into their mouths, while all sorts of wicked things come *out of* their mouths. Now it so happens that Jesus's remarks do attack first of all the oral tradition and then the written Law itself, but this is not the point. What he is talking about is men's habit of observing certain rules while ignoring the real demands of God's will. God's Law requires the giving of money to the temple, but God does not wish this to be done at the expense of care for parents. Similarly the food laws ordain what food God wishes his people to eat, but the scrupulous observance of these laws does not exempt men from keeping themselves 'clean' in another sense.

Whether by saying this Jesus really did mean to nullify the food law is not clear. If his disciples really did eat with unwashed hands and did ignore the rules about purifying cups and dishes, and if he himself really did say 'Nothing that goes into a man from outside can defile him', then we might suppose that he did regard this part of the oral tradition as of no value. But we cannot say for certain. What we do know is that here, as in other areas of Jewish life, he believed it to be vitally important that men should be aware that God's will could not be encompassed by the Law alone, either in its written or in its oral form. It was wrong to observe the Law scrupulously while shutting your eyes to God's greater demands.

'*Love your enemies*'

The Law enjoined the Jew to love members of his own race:

You shall not nurse hatred against your brother . . . You shall not seek revenge, or cherish anger towards your kinsfolk; you shall love your neighbour as a man like yourself. (Lev. 19. 17–18)

On the other hand the 'enemies' of the Jews lay everywhere. There were not only those foreign powers who influenced Israel's fortunes for the worse, but also those Palestinian peoples, most notably the Samaritans, who were not in sympathy with Israelite religion. And Judaism did not lightly forget old grudges:

No Ammonite or Moabite, even down to the tenth generation, shall become a member of the assembly of the Lord . . . because they did not meet you with food and water on your way out of Egypt . . . You shall never seek their welfare or their good all your life long. (Deut. 23. 3–4, 6)

In the face of this cautious hostility to outsiders, Jesus, in the Sermon on the Mount in Matthew's Gospel, is reported to have swept away all distinctions:

You have learned that they were told, 'Love your neighbour, hate your enemy.' But what I tell you is this: Love your enemies and pray for your persecutors . . . (Matt. 5. 43–4; cf. Lk. 6. 27–8, 32–6)

The Sermon on the Mount appears to be a collection of sayings of varying authenticity, and we cannot be certain that anything in it was said in precisely that form by Jesus. Commentators have also objected to this particular passage on the grounds that neither the written Law nor the rabbis told the Jews to hate their enemies. But even if this particular saying is a misrepresentation of traditional Jewish teaching, there can be no doubt that the *implication* of hating one's enemies was to be found in the Law; and it is entirely in keeping with Jesus's behaviour, as we have observed it so far, that he should tell his hearers that simply to obey the Law's command of loving one's kinsfolk is *not enough*: love must be carried further, until even enemies are embraced by it.

In the same context Jesus tells his hearers that the Law's dictum on revenge is similarly inadequate:

You have learned that they were told, 'Eye for eye, tooth for tooth.' But what I tell you is this: Do not set yourself against the man who wrongs you. If someone slaps you on the right cheek, turn and offer him your left. (Matt. 5. 38–9; cf. Lk. 6. 29–30)

Again the commentators point out that the 'revenge' clause in the Law is not so much *demanding* eye for eye and tooth for tooth as *limiting* revenge to this precise redress of the injury, rather than permitting unbridled vengeance. Moreover by the time of Jesus this direct redress had been superseded by a system of payments for injury. But Jesus's dictum is not based on a misapprehension of the Law. He is not, indeed, necessarily even attacking the principle of compensation. What he is saying is that God's will cannot be circumscribed by the compensation rule. God's commands are far greater than this rule suggests. God wishes that men should give all that is demanded of them and still more, however unjust the demand. By the side of this, the mere observation of the Law is inadequate.

Once again, the temptation to the modern mind is to look for some general rule, some moral principle which Jesus is formulating. Indeed it might appear at first sight that one is being offered here. The command to 'love your enemies' and to turn the other cheek has been used to justify pacifism. We should not assume, however, that Jesus was saying that warfare is sinful. He is not offering a rule for general behaviour; he is not (apparently) even thinking of a particular case. What he is doing, once again, is emphasising that God demands more than just the observance of the Law.

The thought is enough

The Jewish Law legislated for men's actions but not for their thoughts. Two instances in the Sermon on the Mount suggest that Jesus considered this to be inadequate.

After quoting the commandment 'Do not commit murder', he continues:

> Anyone who nurses anger against his brother must be brought to judgment . . . If he sneers at him he will have to answer for it in the fires of hell. (Matt. 5. 22)

The mere conceiving of angry thoughts is in God's eyes the equivalent to an act of murder. There is hyperbole here, for Jesus can scarcely mean that in daily life feelings of anger should be punished as if they were murder; this is perhaps why he invokes 'the fires of hell' as an indication of the divine and supernatural punishment, in contrast to the penalties levied by the courts on actual murder. (Whether Jesus envisaged a literal hell-fire for sinners cannot be determined; the words in the original text – 'the gehenna of fire' – refer to the ravine of Gehenna on the outskirts of Jerusalem where the city's offal was burnt, and which was popularly used in Judaism as a symbol of future punishment.) But the moral lesson is clear. In God's eyes it is not enough merely to obey the Law and abstain from the act of murder. For what is murder but the ultimate expression of anger? And in forbidding murder in the Law, God means to forbid not just this ultimate expression but the whole condition of anger, in the mind as well as in outward actions.

Similarly Jesus declares in the Sermon that it is not only the act of adultery, forbidden by the Law, which merits punishment, but the very thinking of lustful thoughts:

If a man looks on a woman with a lustful eye, he has already committed adultery with her in his heart. (Matt. 5. 28)

It would be wrong to suppose that, during all the centuries of Judaism that preceded the teaching of Jesus, nobody had supposed that God demanded inner virtue as well as outward good behaviour. We need look no further than the book of Job in the Old Testament to see that an inner state of mind, such as Job's patience in the face of adversity, was considered to be highly valued by God. It would also be wrong to assume that the antitheses (in the passages on murder–anger and adultery–lust) between the old Law and the teaching of Jesus necessarily represent Jesus's own words. As we have already seen, the Sermon itself is of doubtful authenticity. But there is no doubt that such commands as Jesus is represented as giving here – commands to men to guard their inner thoughts as well as their outward behaviour – are part of his message. The Law, vitally important as it is, does not embrace the whole of God's demands on men. Those demands are universal, total; God demands that the inner man shall obey as well as the outer.

The golden rule

According to one estimate, the rabbinical oral tradition of exegesis of the written Law produced 248 commandments and 365 prohibitions. Even the rabbis were aware that some kind of abbreviation was necessary. It was said that a Gentile once asked the Conservative Shammai how many laws the Jews had, and he replied: 'Two: the oral and the written Law.' Hillel, who as usual was more ready to be free with tradition, said there was only one: 'Do not do to another person what is unwelcome to you: this is the entire Law, and the rest is interpretation.'

It is in the context of this that we should read Jesus's remark near the end of the Sermon on the Mount:

Always treat others as you would like them to treat you: that is the Law and the prophets. (Matt. 7. 12; cf. Lk. 6. 31)

Hillel and he have said almost the same thing. Almost, but not quite. Hillel's precept is negative, Jesus's is positive: Hillel's is a restriction on behaviour, Jesus's an injunction to action.

It is easy for a modern reader to be misled by this 'golden rule' into supposing that Jesus is offering a broad humanistic ethic. Certainly if the golden rule is detached from its context it had this appearance. But Jesus and his fellow Jews were not humanists. They served not man but God, and they did this by obeying the commandments of the Law and the words of the prophets. Undoubtedly many of them did so without questioning *why* any particular commandment should be obeyed; their obedience was blind – and was therefore mechanical, for their intellect was not involved in it. It is a characteristic of Jesus's teaching that he praises not this blind obedience, but the kind of *reasoning* obedience which considers *why* God has given some particular commandment to men. And this is the real meaning of the golden rule. It is a reminder that God's demands on men are not mysterious and impenetrable at all: they will be found to be based on the very simplest of rules, the rule that you should behave towards someone as you would wish to treat yourself. The golden rule is not meant to replace all other rules. It is meant to show men how they can obey God's will whether the Law gives them a specific commandment or not. It is a guiding rule for conduct in those areas – and there are many – where the Law is inadequate, and for cases where different parts of the Law conflict.

Jew, not philosopher

After we have studied those teachings of Jesus which could be called liberal in attitude, it may come as something of a shock to read these words, which Matthew ascribes to him in the Sermon:

> I tell you this: so long as heaven and earth endure, not a letter, not a stroke, will disappear from the Law . . . If any man therefore sets aside even the least of the Law's demands, and teaches others to do the same, he will have the lowest place in the kingdom of Heaven. (Matt. 5. 18–19)

Perhaps Jesus did not express it as strongly as this. Matthew may here be reacting against a streak of 'antinomianism' or moral lawlessness in some parts of the early Christian Church. But maybe Jesus did say just this, and it would not contradict the character of his teaching if he did. For, as should by now be evident, he was not trying to offer new precepts which would supersede the Law. He was encouraging his hearers to give a new interpretation to the word 'Law', to realise that God demands *more* of men than the specific requirements set down in the written Law of Moses and elaborated by the rabbis in the oral tradition. And in doing this he did not negate the value of the Law; rather, he showed that beyond the Law there was (so to speak) a higher law.

What was that higher Law, and how had Jesus come to be aware of it? The answer may seem at first sight banal and misleading; for the truth is that, time after time, the higher law to which Jesus appeals is *men's consciences*. As the modern theologian H. J. Cadbury puts it, after asking how Jesus arrived at his moral judgements:

> Like any other words the words of Jesus find their ultimate sanctions in our own consciences . . . At bottom [there is] a kind of self-validating character in the teachings themselves.

This may seem banal because, after our long search for the source of Jesus's moral judgements, it is a distinct anti-climax to be told that he merely used his conscience, like any modern liberal. And it is misleading because 'conscience' is not a Jewish term. We should not use it to imply that Jesus gave any value to *human* moral judgement. As a Jew, he must have believed that the only moral judge – the only judge of anything – was God. If he thought in terms of anything like a 'conscience', he would presumably have regarded it as the will of God expressing itself clearly in human reason. God was the only judge; but it was wrong to regard the Law as the only mediator of his judgement. His voice spoke clearly in the human mind, for all to hear.

Was this, then, Jesus's distinctive contribution as a teacher? So it will seem to us, though across the gap of centuries we cannot be certain. We might be more definite if we had more contemporary records to show how Jesus compared with other teachers of his time. Certainly the *Mishnah* shows a profound difference of approach between him and the other rabbis, both conservative and liberal; but the *Mishnah*, it must be admitted, is of a later date and only represents one aspect of Judaism, the concern to codify. It is quite possible that there were other religious teachers in the first century whose call to the conscience was much the same as Jesus's. Nor should we be certain that, even if Jesus was distinctive in this respect, it would be this particular feature of his teaching that struck the minds of his hearers as remarkable. As H. J. Cadbury puts it, 'At this distance what seems to us distinctive in Jesus may have been to his hearers commonplace and vice versa.' Cadbury also emphasises that newness, originality – the qualities which the historian is tempted to look for in Jesus – may not have characterised him at all. A great teacher, he suggests, does not so much state things as find remarkable ways of expressing old truths. Cadbury concludes (and we will do well to echo him):

> Perhaps more nearly accurate than the words novel, original, unique, for describing any differentia of Jesus, would be such adjectives as radical, intense, extreme.

So far we have concentrated on what is distinctive about Jesus when he is compared with the rest of Judaism. Does his teaching appear to be so remarkable when it is set against, say, the teachings of Plato and Aristotle? What kind of status should we give to Jesus as a philosopher?

The answer must be that such a comparison is meaningless. Greek philosophy thought in terms of man and his ideals. Of what sort were those ideals, and how should man attain them? Were they, as Plato believed, transcendental Forms towards which the educated man could journey, or was 'good', as Aristotle believed, something to be achieved by moderation and conformity with the laws of nature? It is not just that their conclusions were very different from those of Jesus – though indeed both Plato's paternalistic and totalitarian view of the ideal society and Aristotle's self-sufficient and utterly superior ideal man are as different as they could be from anything that Jesus taught. One fundamental difference is that Plato and Aristotle operated with elaborate philosophical models of man and the world, from which they deduced ethical conclusions. Jesus had no such sophisticated system; his method, if it can be described at all, could be called 'inspirational'. Moreover he did not talk of 'ideals' and 'ethics'. He was concerned with man's *obedience* to God, something which the Greek mind could not imagine; for, as Rudolf Bultmann expresses it, the Greek thinker 'recognizes no authority to which there could be any question of obedience; he knows only the law of the perfecting of his own nature by his achievement'. And – as a final point of comparison – we might note that while the Greek thinkers attempted to produce balanced and consistent ethics, in the manner of a modern moralist, this approach seems to have been foreign to Jesus. There is no concern with consistency in his teaching; he was not preoccupied with the construction of a *system*.

But this radical difference between the approach taken by Jesus and the approach of other Western traditions does not mean that nothing can be extracted from Jesus's teaching that can be understood in terms of non-Jewish moral thought, and be seen as original in such an alien context. The idea that it is the spirit in which someone acts that matters rather than the mere conformity of his action to a set of rules, and the belief that it is the inner thought rather than the outward deed that counts in human affairs, are both central in modern European thought; and it is certainly possible that they can be traced back, at least in part, to the influence of Jesus. In so far as these principles are implicit in what Jesus had to say, it is of course true that, as a Jew, he saw their contribution as being towards greater obedience to God; whereas we may see them rather as vital components of any adequate human ethic. This, though, does not rule out their having had any influence outside the world of Judaistic presuppositions.

Yet Jesus himself, as we have seen, was no philosopher; his mind was characteristically Jewish. Even those of his followers who broke away from Judaism and became Christians did not claim that he had formulated an independent system of ethics. Certainly Paul believed that Jesus had made it no longer necessary for his followers to observe every detail of the Law; in a famous phrase he wrote: 'Christ ends the Law and brings righteousness for everyone who has faith' (Rom. 10. 4). But Paul believed that Jesus had done this not by teaching new things, not indeed by his teaching at all, but by dying on the Cross and rising again. Certainly the early Christian Church came, step by step, to abandon the observation of the Law, concurring with Paul when he said that it had been no more than 'a temporary measure' imposed by God until the coming of Christ (Gal. 3. 19). But this was Paul's and the early Church's view, not Jesus's.

Almost in passing, we have stumbled up against a vital fact. Paul believed that Jesus 'ended' the Law *not because of what he taught but because he died on the Cross*. In other words, from the earliest period of the Christian Church Jesus was regarded as something more than just a teacher. This ought to be apparent simply from the difficulty of identifying what was really characteristic about Jesus's teaching. It would appear from the muddled and often contradictory way in which the early Church preserved that teaching that they did not consider it to be the most remarkable thing about him. Possibly they did not regard it as remarkable at all. What seemed to them to be remarkable was that Jesus was Messiah, Son of Man, Son of God. This was what they believed, and what provided the basis of their allegiance.

But what were Jesus's own ideas about himself? Who did *he* think he was?

5 Who did he think he was?

The Christian Church believed, and on the whole still believes, that the answer to this question is perfectly simple. According to the usual Christian view, Jesus believed, or rather knew, that he was the Messiah – though in rather a special sense, better expressed as 'Son of Man'. His followers gradually realised this, and only the stupidity and downright wickedness of other men prevented them from realising it too during his lifetime.

What is likely to be the truth of this view? And indeed what do these terms, 'Messiah' and 'Son of Man', really mean?

The national Messiah

In chapter 3 we saw how Israel's national ambitions were pushed further and further into the future by continual defeat and failure, so that eventually the simple hope of national triumph was developed into the expectation of an apocalyptic end to the world, after which Israel would at last be made supreme. But not all Jews accepted this. Many clung to the simpler, less supernatural view, and held that a new king David would rise up in their midst, would subdue Israel's enemies and set up his rule in Jerusalem without any end to the present world-order. They constantly looked for the coming of this new David, and frequently thought they had found him. For example, after the return from exile in Babylon in the sixth century B.C. there were many who believed that Zerubbabel the new governor of Jerusalem might be the Messiah; see Zechariah 4. 7: 'How does a mountain, the greatest mountain, compare with Zerubbabel? It is no higher than a plain.' But the hope that Zerubbabel would become a new David came to nothing. Similarly during the second century B.C. the Jewish leader who brought temporary peace with the Syrians, Simon Maccabeus, was regarded by some as having near-Messianic status.

Did Jesus's contemporaries identify him with this national Messiah? Mark would have us believe so. He records that after Jesus has performed many miracles which clearly demonstrate his true nature, he asks the disciples who they think he is, and Peter answers: 'You are the Messiah.' (Mk. 8. 29). Jesus responds by neither admitting nor denying it, but he gives them orders not to tell anyone about it. Some time later, when they reach

Jerusalem, Jesus is hailed by the crowd with the words: 'Blessing on him who comes in the name of the Lord! Blessing on the coming kingdom of our father David!' (Mk. 11. 9–10; cf. Matt. 21. 9; Lk. 19. 38). During the trial of Jesus, the High Priest asks him: 'Are you the Messiah, the Son of the Blessed One?' and Jesus replies, in Mark's version, 'I am' (Mk. 14. 61–2). And at Jesus's crucifixion the accusation against him, fixed over his cross, is summed up in the words: 'The king of the Jews' (Mk. 15. 26; cf. Matt. 27. 37, Lk. 23. 38). Moreover the passers-by taunt him with the words 'Let the Messiah, the king of Israel, come down now from the cross. If we see that, we shall believe' (Mk. 15. 32; cf. Matt. 27. 42, Lk. 23. 37).

Could Jesus really have been making political claims? Could he have regarded himself as the 'king of the Jews' who had come to set Israel free from Roman rule? The idea is certainly not absurd, for no one who stirred up the populace in first-century Palestine could preach a religion which was not felt to be profoundly associated with national ambitions. The coming of the kingdom of God, so closely associated with Jesus's message, would certainly be taken to mean the triumph of Israel. We should not be surprised that some people regarded him as making a political as well as a religious challenge to the existing order. Moreover this is all the more likely to have happened if some of his followers were (as the Gospels say they were) members of the anti-Roman political group which came to be known as the Zealots; see Mark 3. 18 (cf. Matt. 10. 4, Lk. 6. 15), which names one of the disciples as 'Simon of the Zealot party'. But that Jesus himself had any distnctly political ambitions remains in the realm of improbability. The character of his teaching as transmitted by the Church shows nothing of such ambitions, and the Gospels are positive that this was not his own view of himself. They agree (or at least the Synoptics do, for John takes a more sophisticated theological view) that he explicitly renounced political ambitions and instead declared his role to be one of suffering, describing himself as 'Son of Man'.

The Son of Man

The words 'Son of Man' are perhaps the most contentious in the Gospels. Theologians cannot agree precisely what meaning Jesus meant to convey by using them – or indeed whether he intended them to have any special significance at all.

The actual words 'son of man' are a typical Hebrew tautology for 'man', and they were certainly sometimes used to mean merely this. A speaker could refer to himself as 'a son of man' without claiming any sort of title, or saying anything other than 'me'. Some biblical commentators believe that this is all that Jesus meant when he used the expression; they say he was in fact calling himself no more than 'a man' or 'this man'.

On the other hand many commentators believe that Jesus meant the term 'Son of Man' to have distinct theological reverberations. They believe, in fact, that when he spoke of himself in this way he was identifying himself with a messianic-style figure who would usher in the end of the world and God's judgement. The chief ground for believing that this is what Jesus meant is the apparent existence of such a figure in the book of Daniel. Despite its claims to have originated during the Babylonian captivity, 'Daniel' was, as we have seen, actually written not much more than 150 years before the birth of Jesus. Here is the passage from it which describes Daniel's version of the coming of the kingdom of God:

> I saw one like a son of man* coming with the clouds of heaven; he approached the Ancient in Years [i.e. God] and was presented to him. Sovereignty and glory and kingly power were given to him . . . his sovereignty was to be an everlasting sovereignty which should not pass away, and his kingly power such as should never be impaired. (Daniel 7. 13–14)

This passage in Daniel grew out of that strand of Israel's hope for the future which expected a supernatural end of the world rather than a purely this-wordly national triumph. The exact meaning of the passage is far from clear. It is complicated by the fact that the 'son of man' is here certainly something like an allegorical figure, standing for God's faithful people in Israel. Until recently, it was argued by some theologians that there was a ready-made concept of the Son of Man waiting for the author of Daniel to use, and indeed for Jesus to take over. This Son of Man (it was argued) was not a human being at all, despite his name; he was a divine and heavenly creature, created by God before the world was formed; his face shone like an angel and he was endowed with God's miraculous power. Until the coming of the kingdom of God he was being kept hidden in heaven. When the time arrived for the kingdom to come he would descend to earth accompanied by the 'clouds of heaven'. His coming would be like lightning, and he would summon all the nations to be judged by himself as

* The New English Bible actually reads 'I saw one like a man', but the literal meaning of the Hebrew is 'one like a son of man'.

God's representative. This judgement of the living would be accompanied by the resurrection of the dead, who would themselves be judged. The righteous, or more particularly the righteous Israelites, would be delivered into eternal bliss and would be given authority in the kingdom of God; all other nations would fall at their feet, and at the feet of the Son of Man, whom they would worship.

But nowadays there is a great deal of doubt about this. Did such a precise concept of the Son of Man really exist for Jesus to take over, or were the words 'son of man' in truth a great deal more ambiguous than this interpretation would suggest? Certainly there are Jewish texts which do describe the Son of Man on exactly these terms, but they are of doubtful date, and it would be unwise to assume that Jesus and his contemporaries knew them and agreed with them in their use of the term 'son of man'. We do know that Jesus was well acquainted with the Daniel passage – the book of Daniel was very highly regarded in his day. But if he was referring to the Daniel 'son of man' when he called himself by this title, we cannot say precisely what he meant, so ambiguous is the Daniel passage; and anyway we have no certainty that on every occasion when Jesus used the words 'Son of Man' he meant to refer to the Daniel passage at all.

In order to find some way out of this labyrinth, we need to look at the various ways in which the Synoptic Gospels use the term Son of Man (John usually prefers simply 'the Son', implying the Son of God). In all, the Synoptics employ it nearly seventy times, though of course many of these are parallel reports of the same incidents. It is quite an illuminating exercise to divide their uses of the term into categories.

First, there are the passages where the words 'Son of Man' certainly refer to the Daniel passage. The most notable of these is this episode in the trial of Jesus. This is how Mark narrates it:

> Again the High Priest questioned him: 'Are you the Messiah, the Son of the Blessed One?' Jesus said, 'I am; and you will see the Son of Man seated at the right hand of God and coming with the clouds of heaven.' (Mk. 14. 61–2)

Matthew presents it like this:

> 'Are you the Messiah, the Son of God?' Jesus replied, 'The words are yours. But I tell you this: from now on, you will see the Son of Man seated at the right hand of God and coming on the clouds of heaven.' (Matt. 26. 63–4; cf. Lk. 2. 67–70)

Two other passages where a reference to Daniel is implied record

Jesus as expecting this coming of the Son of Man to happen very soon. He says to his disciples:

> I tell you this: there are some standing here who will not taste death before they have seen the Son of Man coming in his kingdom. (Matt. 16. 28; cf. Mk. 9. 1, Lk. 9. 27)

Indeed Matthew actually records Jesus as promising the coming of the Son of Man with the kingdom of God in a matter of months or weeks rather than years; Matthew's version of the instruction to the disciples before they go off on an independent mission includes these words of Jesus:

> I tell you this: before you have gone through all the towns of Israel the Son of Man will have come. (Matt. 10. 23)

How likely is it that these implied references to Daniel are the authentic words of Jesus? We cannot say for certain. But certainly Jesus's alleged answer to the High Priest during his trial does seem rather odd when considered in its context. Up to this point in the narrative Jesus has refused to be goaded by his accusers into making any claims about himself. Now he suddenly declares himself to be Son of Man. We may in fact suspect that the words have been included (in what was after all a highly conjectural report of what may have occurred at the trial) simply to allow Jesus a moment of glory in the face of his accusers, and to give clear grounds for his condemnation. But as to the other passages where Jesus predicts the nearness of his coming as Son of Man, it is certainly hard to explain why they should have been included if they were not based on real sayings of Jesus. By the time the Gospels were written the prediction of a very swift coming of the Son of Man – 'before you have gone through all the towns of Israel' – had proved untrue, and undoubtedly many of Jesus's original disciples had died, so that the prediction that some of them would live to see the coming of the kingdom must have at least seemed open to question. It is hard, therefore, to see how these passages could have been pure invention. Very possibly they are authentic reflections of Jesus's belief that the kingdom would come soon. On the other hand their very confident character contrasts oddly with another passage where he says that the date of the coming of the kingdom simply cannot be foretold:

> But about that day or that hour no one knows, not even the angels in heaven, not even the Son; only the Father. (Mk. 13. 32; cf. Matt. 24. 36)

Altogether we would be unwise to put too much weight on any of these passages if we are trying to prove that Jesus regarded himself as Son of Man in a Daniel sense.

Certainly there are also a number of other places where he is reported as referring to the glorious coming of the Son of Man; these are found in the 'apocalyptic' or visionary discourse with which all three Synoptics preface the Passion (Mark chapter 13, Matthew chapters 24–5, Luke chapter 21). Here, Jesus talks of events which are to come after his death: false prophets, wars, rumours of the end of the world, earthquakes, the persecution of his followers, and (perhaps, though this is not clear) the fall of Jerusalem in A.D. 70. This speech contains several references to the 'coming' of the Son of Man. But is it authentic? While one or two commentators think so, the general view is that it is the work of a later writer or tradition, and certainly it is very much in the style of other Jewish–Christian apocalyptic books.

These, then, are the sayings in the Gospels where Jesus is definitely represented as referring to the Daniel-style Son of Man. And it is a case of 'referring to', not 'identifying with', for the fact is that all these sayings are in the third person. Jesus never declares unambiguously 'I am the Son of Man', and very often he could be talking about a third party:

> ... They will see the Son of Man coming in the clouds with great power and glory ... (Mk. 13. 26)

> Hold yourself ready, therefore, because the Son of Man will come at the time you least expect him. (Matt. 24. 44)

> ... everyone who acknowledges me before men, the Son of Man will acknowledge before the angels of God ... (Lk. 12. 8)

It is only a presumption that Jesus is here talking about himself. No doubt the writers of the Gospels thought he was, but were they in fact recording sayings in which he had meant to refer not to himself – about whom he was here making no claims – but to the divine being who would eventually usher in the kingdom of God, a being with whom he did not identify himself? This is certainly a possibility.

We come now to the other category of 'Son of Man' sayings in the Gospels: those where Jesus is not so certainly referring to the Daniel concept. In none of these passages is he obviously claiming any special title for himself – rather he might simply be using a commonplace circumlocution for 'mankind' or 'myself'. For example:

> The Sabbath was made for the sake of man and not man for the Sabbath: therefore the Son of Man is sovereign even over the Sabbath. (Mk. 2. 27–8)

We can certainly take this to mean '*mankind* is sovereign even over the Sabbath' – an extension of the first part of the precept. In another passage which falls into this category, Jesus is certainly referring to himself when he says 'Son of Man', but he may mean no more than 'me':

> 'We are now going to Jerusalem,' he said; 'and the Son of Man will be given up to the chief priests and the doctors of the law; they will condemn him to death and hand him over to the foreign power. He will be mocked and spat upon, flogged and killed; and three days afterwards, he will rise again.' (Mk. 10. 33–4; cf. Matt. 20. 18–19, Lk. 18. 31–3)

It ought to be mentioned that most commentators find it impossible to believe that these are the authentic words of Jesus; if he had told his disciples so plainly what was to happen, they would hardly have been cast into despondency by his death, and have been astonished by reports of his resurrection, as the Gospels say they were. But even if the passage were authentic, there is no reason to suppose that the words 'Son of Man' in it – and indeed in the two other very similar predictions of the Passion (Mk. 8. 31, 9. 30–2 and parallels in Matt. and Lk.) – need to be taken to mean more than 'I myself', 'this man'.

On the other hand it is difficult to imagine that the writers of the Gospels, and the many members of the early Church who preserved the traditions on which the Gospels were based, believed that Jesus was making no special claim for himself when he used the term 'Son of Man'. If they had thought the words meant no more than 'I myself', would they have troubled to record them so often? Or can we suppose that every instance of the words 'Son of Man' in the Gospels is an invention by the Church? It is possible, but unlikely. The connotations of the phrase were so vague – far more vague than 'Messiah' – that it seems an improbable thing for anyone to invent totally. It would be more reasonable to suppose that Jesus used the term often enough to impress his hearers. We simply cannot say for certain what he means by it; though we can guess.

The Suffering Servant

Before we make our guess, we need to look at another view which Jesus may have held about himself. Neither the Jewish national Messiah nor the 'one like a son of man' in the book of Daniel had any suggestion of suffering about them; they were both glorious figures, the victors, not the vanquished. Yet the Gospels portray Jesus as associating his role as Messiah or Son of Man – and note how both terms appear side by side here – with suffering:

> ... he asked his disciples, 'Who do men say I am?' ... Peter replied: 'You are the Messiah.' Then he gave them strict orders not to tell anyone about him; and he began to teach them that the Son of Man had to undergo great sufferings, and to be rejected by the elders, chief priests, and doctors of the law; to be put to death ... (Mk. 8. 27–31)

The prophetic element in this passage makes many commentators doubt its authenticity. But even if Jesus did not predict his sufferings in the very literal way depicted by the Gospels, it is not unreasonable to suppose, from the manner in which he seems to have gone to his death, that he believed that by suffering he could in some way make 'atonement', that is, effect a reconciliation between God and man, even 'take away the sins of the world'. Theologians are especially inclined to believe this because of the existence of such a concept in the Jewish scriptures which Jesus knew so well.

The passages in question are all in the book of Isaiah, though modern commentators believe them to be the work neither of Isaiah himself nor even of 'Second Isaiah', but of a third writer or school of writers. These passages are in the form of poems, which have been absorbed into the text of Isaiah. The first three of these poems or 'Servant Songs' (as they are now known) tell of the call of a prophet who is to bring Israel back to the worship of Yahweh; he is also to be 'a light to the nations', a preacher to the whole world (Is. 42. 1–4, 49. 1–6, 50. 4–11). But it is the fourth Song which concerns us most. Set in the past tense, it tells of the Servant's miserable life on earth. He was, says the poet, physically unattractive, even hideous, and despised. Moreover he suffered from a foul disease which gave him great agonies. Yet this suffering was a positive element in the work to which he was called. It was in fact a suffering of atonement:

> ... on himself he bore our sufferings,
>   our torments he endured,
> while we counted him smitten by God,
>   struck down by disease and misery;
> but he was pierced for our transgressions,
>   tortured for our iniquities;
> the chastisement he bore is health for us,
>   and by his scourging we are healed.

We had all strayed like sheep,
  each of us had gone his own way;
but the Lord laid upon him
  the guilt of us all. (Is. 53. 4–6)

The Servant endured other sufferings too: he died the death of a criminal, and was given an ignominious burial. But the poem ends with the assurance that Yahweh will give the Servant his reward and will show the world his true greatness. He will in fact raise the Servant from the dead, bringing him back to earthly life so that he will 'enjoy long life and see his children's children' (Is. 53. 10). Yahweh declares:

. . . I will allot him a portion with the great,
  and he shall share the spoil with the mighty,
because he exposed himself to face death
  and was reckoned among transgressors,
because he bore the sin of many
  and interceded for their transgressions. (Is. 53. 12)

The interpretation of these poems is not easy, but it seems most likely that they were based on a real historical person, a prophet whose personal sufferings were regarded as an atonement for the sins of Israel. A belief in some kind of 'sympathetic' suffering was certainly held by a number of prophets, such as Isaiah himself, who was recorded to have walked naked and barefoot for three years in order to bring down the same disgrace on the Ethiopians and Egyptians, and Jeremiah, who walked about with an iron yoke on his neck in order to illustrate and bring to pass the fate which awaited Judah, slavery under the 'yoke' of Babylon. Many prophets indeed regarded the character of their whole lives as a 'sign' of this kind. Jeremiah was forbidden to marry and was made to cut himself off from society, while Ezekiel was obliged to undergo physical sufferings as an emblem of the impending ruin of Jerusalem. In this sense the Servant Songs are part of a wider tradition.

On the other hand the tradition of prophetic sufferings did not specifically involve atonement, the notion that such sufferings might be accepted by God as a kind of ransom for Israel's sins. And this idea is explicitly present in the Servant Songs. It is true that atonement was not exactly an unusual idea in Jewish thought: the sacrifices in the temple at Jerusalem implied it. But the notion of a man dying on behalf of the whole nation's sins is found most notably in the Servant Songs, so that if Jesus really believed that his own suffering and death was an offering for the sins of men he was probably deriving this idea from these Songs.

This is what more conservative theologians think he was doing. They believe that he united with the title 'Son of Man' the concept of the Suffering Servant. He believed, they think, that the kingdom of God would be ushered in not just by a cosmic crisis but by his own suffering on the cross, which would atone for the sins of men. In other words, according to this view Jesus believed of himself what the Christian Church came to believe about him: that his death – followed by his resurrection – was itself the great event through which God declared his mercy to mankind. In a sense it even took the place of the coming of the kingdom, or was at least the first stage in the kingdom's arrival on earth.

The great appeal of this view of the historical Jesus is that it harmonises with the Church's later conceptions of him. On the other hand it certainly does not fit the evidence very comfortably. In the Synoptic Gospels there is only one passage where Jesus explicitly associates his death with atonement or 'ransom':

> Jesus called them [the disciples] to him and said, 'You know that in the world the recognised rulers lord it over their subjects . . . That is not the way with you; among you, whoever wants to be great must be your servant . . . For even the Son of Man did not come to be served but to serve, and to give up his life as a ransom for many.' (Mk. 10. 42–5; cf. Matt. 20. 25–8)

If Jesus said this, there could be no doubt that he believed that his death on the cross would have an atoning power. But did he say it? One isolated instance seems a slender peg on which to hang so much, particularly as by the time the Gospels were written the Church had certainly developed its own ideas about the crucifixion as an atonement. Most commentators suspect that these words were not spoken by Jesus. (It should be noted that Luke does not include the reference to 'ransom' in his version of the episode.) Yet many who reject the authenticity of this particular passage still assume that Jesus did believe that his death was (or might be) a vicarious sacrifice offered to God on behalf of the sins of men. Is this view justified?

Moralist or miracle worker?

A historian must surely judge the evidence we have examined to be inconclusive. The Gospels indicate that Jesus did not regard himself as the national Messiah of popular Jewish hopes, but they do not allow us to come to any firm conclusions as to whether he used the words 'Son of Man' as a title for himself, or precisely what he meant by it if he did. Nor do they allow us to say for certain that he regarded his death as having an atoning power, like the death of the Suffering Servant in Isaiah. We are therefore obliged, if we are going to come to any conclusions, to consider other aspects of the issue: we need to ask whether it is psychologically and historically probable that Jesus should have made these claims about himself.

If we judge the psychological issue in purely twentieth-century terms the answer will probably be 'no'. To modern minds it seems that if Jesus did believe himself to be Son of Man (in the sense of God's vicegerent, sent from heaven), then he must have been quite astonishingly self-assured. Could he really believe that he was a divine being who would one day descend to earth on the clouds of heaven and rule in glory? The modern theologian John Knox asks if it would be 'psychologically possible for a sane person' to think this, and says: 'For myself, I find it exceedingly hard to answer affirmatively.' And to the modern observer's way of thinking, even if Jesus's conception of his role chiefly involved suffering rather than glory – even if, in other words, he thought he was merely the Suffering Servant – was he not still making an immense claim? Knox again finds such a claim incompatible with Jesus's sanity, or at least his modesty; how, he asks, *could* Jesus have believed that his own death could 'take away the sins of the world'? However steeped he may have been in the book of Isaiah, however much he may have been influenced by the Jewish sacrificial outlook, why should he think that he himself was to be the man sacrificed on behalf of all? To Knox, and to our way of thinking in general (if we make no effort to project ourselves back into the first century's beliefs), it would have been a vast, an insane claim.

But while Knox's view makes sense in the twentieth century, it is of doubtful relevance to the period of history we are discussing. Given the culture of Jesus's day, people could certainly entertain ideas about themselves which we would regard as insane. The prophets of ancient Israel had made claims about their authority as God's mouthpiece which were, it seems, often accepted; and we may suppose that in Jesus's time for a man to suggest he was the Messiah would not be an utterly outrageous idea. Certainly in the troubled period of Jewish history which followed Jesus's death a number of messianic claimants appeared, most notably Bar Cochba ('Son of the Star'), who led a revolt against the Romans in A.D. 132–5. He claimed to be Messiah, and was widely accepted as such. This is not to say that there would be nothing extraordinary in such claims – witness the outrage of the High Priest when Jesus, during his trial, apparently claimed to be Son of Man in the Daniel sense. But we should not assume that a messianic view of himself would be incompatible with Jesus's sanity.

It ought to be emphasised that Jesus's manner of speaking seems to have been very different from the manner either of the rabbis or of the ancient prophets. The rabbis, as we have seen, took their authority from the exegesis of the written Law, and from the doctrine of their own teachers, which was ultimately derived (they believed) from Moses, and so from God himself. The great prophets of ancient Israel, on the other hand, had claimed to be the direct mouthpiece of God; they often prefaced their sayings with the words 'Thus says the Lord'. Jesus fits into neither of these patterns. At times he does use scriptural exegesis, for instance in his dispute with the Pharisees about the Sabbath (Mk. 2. 25–6). But this is comparatively unusual, and his most characteristic utterances are not primarily based on scriptural interpretation. As to the prophetic style of utterance, he is never recorded as using the words 'Thus says the Lord', or indeed anything like them. This is the sort of manner in which the Gospels recorded him as introducing his teachings:

I tell you this . . . (Mk. 3. 28 and *passim*)

Take note of what you hear . . . (Mk. 4. 24)

Listen to me, all of you . . . (Mk. 7. 14)

(And there are many examples in Matthew's and Luke's Gospels.) The phrase 'I tell you this', or, as earlier translations of the Bible render it, 'Verily I say unto you', appears to have been Jesus' characteristic way of introducing his precepts. If it was, then certainly nothing like it is found elsewhere in Judaism, and the startling effect of the words '*I* tell you' on the ears of pious Jews can hardly be exaggerated. That a man should simply claim to have personal authority for making the kind of statements that Jesus made, and should not derive them from the Law and the Prophets, or at least maintain that they were the words of God communicated through prophetic utterance, was tantamount to heresy. So what prompted Jesus to regard himself as having such authority?

A philosopher might ask if he in fact needed any authority to make the kind of ethical statement he made. Was it necessary to (as it were) show any credentials before telling people to behave to others as you would wish them to behave to you, to love your enemies, to give your money to the poor? One might suppose such moral lessons as these to be self-evident. Indeed we have already admitted that Jesus's moral teachings *are* self-evident, self-justifying, or at least that they agree precisely with what most of us find in what we call our consciences. And for this reason the theologian H. J. Cadbury doubts whether Jesus did in fact introduce them in the manner recorded by the Gospels. Cadbury suspects that 'I tell you this' was not his usual habit of speech, but was introduced in the Gospels so as to contrast his teaching with the Law (see the Sermon on the Mount in Matthew, where it certainly has this function). Cadbury writes:

> I think he expected his hearers to rely more on themselves than on himself. At least once he says this explicitly, expostulating with them, 'Why don't you judge *even of yourselves* what is right?'

If Cadbury is right, this leaves us with a Jesus who states self-evident moral truth by calling on his hearers to look into their own consciences. He may have done this. But – as Cadbury himself emphasises – if he did, then there must have been some special reason why people listened to him.

If a man were to get up in the twentieth century and preach a moral message whose kernel was 'You will find the truth in your consciences', he would scarcely command a large audience – unless there was something particularly remarkable about him. How much more, then, must this have been true of first-century Palestine, where there was a tradition of prophetic utterance (albeit a lapsed tradition), and a universal belief in the supernatural. Jesus's moral teaching (as we have it) does not in itself explain the degree of attention he attracted. We simply do not find in it sufficient reason for his being put to death, and for a new religion of enormous power to grow up around his person. The 'liberal Protestant' picture of Jesus as a modest moral teacher may be attractive to us, but such a figure would have cut little ice in the context of first-century Judaism.

How, then, do we explain the impact of Jesus and of the ideas behind his teaching? We are led towards one obvious conclusion – a conclusion which is extremely uncomfortable for most twentieth-century minds, even for many twentieth-century Christians. As H. J. Cadbury puts it, 'Jesus's teaching gained prestige from his miracles. There can be little doubt of that.'

6 The miraculous kingdom

The Gospels say very clearly that Jesus performed miracles. They report that he healed the chronically sick, gave sight to the blind and hearing to the deaf, and even brought dead people back to life. They also tell stories of other physical wonders: how he calmed a storm on the Lake of Galilee by the force of his words, how he walked on the water, and how he fed many thousands of people with just a few small loaves of bread and a handful of fishes. How are we to judge such things?

The first point to note is that there are rational explanations of how the stories may have arisen. The account of Jesus miraculously stilling the storm (Mk. 4. 35–41, Matt. 8. 32–7, Lk. 8. 22–5) could have grown out of the Jewish belief that the ability to control the sea and to subdue tempests was a characteristic sign of divine power – see Psalm 89. 9, where God is described as ruling the sea and 'calming the turmoil of its waves', and also the opening verses of Genesis, where the waters represent uncreated chaos. In a rather different way the Old Testament may also have influenced the growth of the story of the Feeding of the Five Thousand (Mk. 6. 30–44, Matt. 14. 13–21, Lk. 9. 10–17, Jn. 6. 1–13). Possibly Jesus concluded an open-air sermon at which a large crowd was present by distributing to each person a fragment of bread as a sign of fellowship with him and God, and in the disciples' memories (or in later tradition) this became an actual meal at which the participants were fully fed by miraculous means – an echo, in fact, of the miraculous feeding of the Israelites in the desert, after they had come out of Egypt, when God sent 'manna' from heaven to sustain them (Ex. 16. 1 ff.).

Certainly where the healing miracles of Jesus are concerned there is much to support the theory that the Gospels told stories about Jesus casting out devils because that is what early Jewish Christians assumed he must have done. The very nature of the kingdom of God, of which they believed him to be a part, was such that its manifestation on earth would be accompanied by events of this kind. When God came into his kingly power in the world he would (the Jews believed) crush the powers of evil and drive them out. That there were powers of evil to be driven out was actually a recent Jewish belief, dating from about the time of the exile in Babylon, when notions about the powers of good and evil being perpetually at war began to infiltrate Jewish thought from Persian religion. By the time of Jesus these notions were embedded deeply in the Jewish imagination. Earlier, the general attitude to sickness had been that it was a punishment from God, and this belief survived into the first century A.D., but it had been largely displaced by the notion that many diseases were actually caused by a devil taking possession of the sufferer. And so it came to be believed that, when the kingdom of God dawned and all evil spirits were driven from their hiding-places to be destroyed, many sick people would consequently be cured of their maladies. It is this which explains the behaviour (as reported in the Gospels) of the demons whom Jesus casts out. Mark in particular is always reporting that they *recognise* Jesus and are frightened because he is 'the Holy One of God' who has come to destroy them (e.g. Mk. 1. 24). The fact that in this process of driving-out a number of men and women are healed of their afflictions interests Mark rather less.

So we might suggest that Mark – or more accurately the oral tradition that he recorded – actually invented these healing miracles so as to portray Jesus driving out devils and thus showing himself to be the Messiah, the agent of the kingdom of God. There is probably an element of truth in this, perhaps a large element. On the other hand a number of the stories of healing miracles say nothing whatever about devils. For example:

They came to Jericho; and as he was leaving the town, with his disciples and a large crowd, Bartimaeus son of Timaeus, a blind beggar, was seated at the roadside. Hearing that it was Jesus of Nazareth, he began to shout, 'Son of David, Jesus, have pity on me!' Many of the people told him to hold his tongue; but he shouted all the more, 'Son of David, have pity on me.' Jesus stopped and said, 'Call him'; so they called the blind man and said, 'Take heart; stand up; he is calling you.' At that he threw off his cloak, sprang up, and came to Jesus. Jesus said to him, 'What do you want me to do for you?' 'Master', the blind man answered, 'I want my sight back.' Jesus said to him, 'Go; your faith has cured you.' And at once he recovered his sight and followed him on the road. (Mk. 10. 46–52; cf. Matt. 20. 29–34, Lk. 18 35–43)

It is very likely that stories such as this were influenced by the belief, undoubtedly held by early Christians, that Jesus must have fulfilled such Old Testament prophecies as the passage in Isaiah (42. 18) which promised the giving of sight to the blind. Moreover the Bartimaeus story has symbolic meanings: though Bartimaeus is blind he recognises Jesus as 'Son of David'

(Messiah), and when he recovers his sight he 'follows' Jesus, that is, has the spiritual insight to recognise him as Lord. The story also shows how true faith can triumph over all adversity. No doubt these layers of symbolic meaning made the story very useful for preachers in the early Church. Quite possibly indeed the early Church invented it, and many other stories of the same kind, for preaching purposes. Such invention would have taken place gradually. For example, in the earliest days of preaching there might merely be generalised statements about Jesus being able to do wonderful things. A little later, more specific claims might be made, such as 'He could do anything: he could even give sight to the blind and hearing to the deaf.' Later still, a real memory of Jesus giving some sort of help to a beggar at Jericho might become the story of Jesus curing him of blindness.

Undoubtedly this kind of process did occur. Anyone who has collected material for a biography will know how often those close to its subject – his friends and even his family – will unconsciously depart from the strict historical truth in their recollections, even a few years after the events, let alone some decades later. The tendency is to adapt real memories until they are formulated into neat anecdotes with a beginning and end and a distinct point or moral to them. These anecdotes are usually based on some sort of truth, but often only very shakily. That this should happen to recollections of Jesus in the disciples' minds is surely inevitable, especially as they were recounting those memories in order to make claims about what he had done. Moreover many of those who preached about Jesus had never known him when he was alive on earth. Indeed the person who still doubts whether such invention really did take place need only listen to modern sermons. Sooner or later he will hear a preacher making statements about the life and ministry of Jesus which cannot be borne out word by word by the Gospels. Invention did, and does, take place, albeit unconsciously. On the other hand the historian cannot determine precisely where it has operated, and to what extent. He can only have his suspicions, or make allegations. He can prove nothing.

Where the healing miracles are concerned, he would also do well to avoid the kind of rationalisation in which some nineteenth-century writers indulged, such as the suggestion that Jesus had a private supply of mysterious drugs and ointments which produced miraculous cures. There is rather less absurdity in the notion that Jesus realised that many of those who begged for help were psychosomatic sufferers who could be healed merely through their own faith in the cure and in the power of the healer. Yet could this really be applied to all those whom Jesus is said to have cured—epileptics, paralytics, lepers, the blind and the deaf?

We may note, when trying to explain the miracle stories, that such things had featured in Jewish legend for many centuries. It was recorded that Moses caused the waters of the Red Sea to move aside and let the Israelites pass in safety, and that Elijah raised a widow's son from death and summoned fire down from heaven on an altar. The Old Testament is full of such stories. Moreover the holy man who was said to work miraculous cures and control the elements was not an entirely uncommon figure in the time of Jesus. For example, Honi the Circle-Drawer was said to have brought rain to end a drought, and Hanina ben Dosa supposedly worked miraculous cures, some of them, like the cures of Jesus, being performed at a distance from the sufferer. This indicates that Jesus's reputation as a miracle-worker, healer and exorcist was by no means unique even in the first century A.D. It was part of the vocabulary of the time for expressing how remarkable someone was.

But this does not mean that we can dismiss the miracles as a totally fictitious part of the Gospels; or at least, if we do this we are rejecting an enormous and highly distinctive part of the tradition about Jesus. If we label the miraculous element as fiction and discuss Jesus purely in terms of his teachings we may be satisfying the demands of those modern minds which do not accept the supernatural, but we are doing violence to the historical record. We are also leaving ourselves with a 'non-miraculous' Jesus whose extraordinary impact on his contemporaries becomes inexplicable. His teachings on their own are not enough to explain the impression he caused. A more honest historian will say that undoubtedly the miracle stories in their present form include a large element of elaboration and invention; but he will also say that something happened which gave rise to those stories. He will also suggest that it was this 'something', this 'wonder-worker' element in Jesus, which gave authority to his teaching. People listened to him because they were astonished by what he did.

But what did he do? What would we have seen if we had been there? We simply cannot say, because we can only study what happened during Jesus's ministry by reading accounts of it written by people with a very different outlook from that of the twentieth-century historian. Jesus's observers believed in a God who had intervened directly in history with miraculous actions, and would do so again. They believed in devils who inhabited the bodies of men, and who could be cast out by an agent of God. They believed that persons acting as God's representatives, such as the prophet Elijah, had already raised dead people to life, and that this could happen again. Their presuppositions were, in other words, entirely and utterly different from the presuppositions of a modern rationalist. Whatever happened during Jesus's ministry, they saw it against this background, and their account of it was based on these beliefs. If we had been there, we might have come to very different conclusions. We (with *our* presuppositions) might have talked not about miracles but about psychosomatic cures and the remarkable impact of a charismatic personality. We might have seen not supernatural events but the reactions of supernaturally-minded people, who were deeply impressed by a man who behaved as if he were the agent of God.

For Jesus believed all these things too: we must not forget that. He was no modern rationalist. He shared the beliefs of his contemporaries, and if they believed that he could perform miracles it seems highly likely that he believed it too. This is not to say that he necessarily presented himself in public primarily as a miracle-worker; the indications are rather the opposite. He is never reported as discussing the miracles; rather, his usual habit is to try to persuade people to keep quiet about them – 'He gave them strict orders to let no one hear about it' (Mk. 5. 43) is his typical reaction after performing a miraculous cure. This may be explained by Mark's belief that Jesus simply wished to keep his messianic status a secret, something that Mark is always emphasising in his Gospel. But it might also reflect that Jesus was himself startled or overawed by whatever cures he did perform. He certainly does not seem to have wished to advertise his powers. Yet we should not suppose from this that he did not believe in the cures, and perhaps in other miraculous events too. The indications are that, in this respect at least, the modern rationalist would have found him a very uncongenial figure: a supernaturalist, a believer, in fact, in his own miraculous powers, a thoroughly Jewish and first-century figure, not a twentieth-century liberal Protestant at all; certainly 'a man for others' (as he has sometimes been called), but also somebody who believed himself to be the special agent of God.

For we may guess, from the dominant role played by the miracles in the Gospels, and from the constant emphasis on Jesus's messianic status and his alleged use, time after time, of the words

'Son of Man', that he did not reject all suggestions that he was some kind of Messiah, but admitted, if only tacitly, that he had been in some way specially appointed by God for the furtherance of the coming of the kingdom. He seems to have rejected any identification of himself with the national, political Messiah; but we may well suppose that he did adopt the term 'Son of Man' to describe himself, perhaps because of the very ambiguity which puzzled us when we discussed its use as a title. He must surely have realised that it evoked echoes of 'one like a son of man' in Daniel, but that on the other hand it could also be taken as nothing more than a tautology for 'myself'. It may have seemed to him that this imprecise term was an ideal title for him to use in a ministry which was quite unlike anything previously known in Judaism, and which perhaps surprised even him in the dramatic turns it took. But that he felt he had some special relationship to God, some messianic role or 'sonship' which manifested itself in miracles and gave powerful authority to his teaching, we cannot doubt. Moreover his teaching itself was largely concerned with the miraculous, with the wholly marvellous and inexplicable power of God and his kingdom: this emerges clearly from the area of Jesus's teaching which we have so far neglected, the parables.

Why Jesus taught in parables

The Gospels record that Jesus taught largely in parables, vivid stories designed to express an idea or to illustrate a point; and there is no reason to doubt this. It was a common method of teaching among the rabbis, as can be seen from the *Talmud* ('teaching'), the chief work of the Jewish post-Biblical literature. This does not mean, of course, that Jesus told precisely those parables that the Gospels record him as telling. Many of the parables found in Matthew and Luke do not appear in Mark's text, and while they may have been derived from reliable sources there is always the possibility that they are inventions, perhaps even compositions of Matthew and Luke themselves. For example a number of the best-known parables – the Good Samaritan, the Lost Sheep, the Lost Coin, the Prodigal Son, the Unjust Steward, Dives and Lazarus—appear in Luke's Gospel alone, a fact which must raise doubts about their authenticity, though they certainly reflect the spirit of Jesus's teaching (Lk. 10. 30–7, 15. 3–16, 13, 16. 19–31). So we must, as usual, exercise caution. On the other hand we may decide to accept at least the outline of some of the parables as reflecting the real teachings of

Jesus, especially those parables which appear in all three Synoptic Gospels and which deal with the central issue of his mission, the kingdom of God. Indeed these 'parables of the kingdom', as they are usually called, would seem to be crucial to Jesus's teaching, since they are the only substantial sayings of Jesus which Mark includes in his Gospel.

Why should Jesus apparently have set much of his teaching in the form of parables? Mark answers this very oddly to modern ears, by saying that Jesus chose the parabolic method because he wanted his teaching to be understood only by his close followers; he used parables (says Mark) to cloak his meaning and confuse the rest of his audience (Mk. 4. 10–12; cf. Matt. 13. 10–12, Lk. 8. 9–10). We are unlikely to accept this as a true account of Jesus's motives. It would be strange that Jesus, preaching in public, should want to confuse his audience deliberately. The passage in Mark also shows the influence of the 'gnostic' type of religion, whose initiates believe they have a *gnosis* or secret knowledge which is denied to others, and though 'gnosticism' seems to have appealed to Mark there is no reason to suppose he is recording a trait in the historical Jesus. Mark's explanation of Jesus teaching in parables is also motivated by his doctrine of the 'messianic secret', his notion that Jesus was not universally recognised as Messiah because he kept his messianic status concealed.

If we reject Mark's account of why Jesus used parables, what is the real explanation? Perhaps it is the very opposite of what Mark suggests. Jesus was preaching for much of the time not to educated intellectuals but to the common people, especially the poor and outcast. His audience's attention could be best held by telling them stories. Statements about the kingdom of God would attract notice more easily if they were set in picture language. So he chose the imagery of daily life in Galilee – the farmer sowing, the vineyard owner hiring his labourers, the crops springing up in the field – to picture the workings of the kingdom.

Indeed there is every reason to suppose that this was Jesus's own mode of thinking. Very probably he himself was not highly educated, and we should not expect his mind to work exclusively in abstractions. Obviously he was capable of clear thought and reasoning; his disputes with the Pharisees (if they represent historical conversations) show a very nimble mind at work, a mind quite capable of dealing with learned people. But we may suspect that for much of the time he himself thought in parables.

Nevertheless there remains the fact that, though the parables are simply stories, their precise meaning is often far from clear. This is not just because of the passage of time between Jesus and ourselves; Mark says that the disciples themselves had to ask Jesus to explain the parables because they did not understand them (Mk. 4. 10).

This difficulty is greatest with many of the short figurative sayings ascribed to Jesus, a large proportion of which have become detached from their original contexts. For example, all three Synoptic Gospels report Jesus as saying something on the lines of 'Salt is a good thing; but if the salt lose its saltiness, what will you season it with?' (Mk. 9. 50). But none of the three agrees with the others either on the saying's place in Jesus's ministry or on its precise meaning. They record it so as to give it both a different context and a different emphasis (Matt. 5. 13, Lk. 14. 34–5). The meaning obviously depended on the precise circumstances in which the saying was uttered.

Indeed it is not just these shorter sayings that present problems of interpretation. In many parables, while the general meaning may be clear the significance of the various details of the story is not at all clear. An example is the parable of the Sower (Mk. 4. 3–9), where the footpath, the birds and the sun do not have any obvious significance. For a time it was fashionable in theological circles to say that if only we could recover the precise circumstances in which the parables were told by Jesus – the 'life situation' or *Sitz im Leben* as Form-critics in Germany have called it – we would understand exactly what he meant.

But would we? Very often we are probably looking for too close a correspondence between the details of the parables and the precise details of Jesus's message. Many parables probably contain no more than a broad general meaning; they are not detailed allegories at all. And besides, in our careful search for the correct interpretation of each parable, are we not perhaps missing the point? Might it not be true that at least some of the parables have no precise abstract meaning at all? Might Jesus not have taught in parables because he himself could not express in any other way what he was trying to say?

The miraculous kingdom

Jesus's task was to preach about the kingdom of God. But he did not do this in purely abstract terms, for he had a conception of it which did not communicate itself so much to the intellect as to the imagination. He did not say 'The kingdom of God *is* so-and-so', but 'The kingdom of God is *like* such-and-such'. Indeed in many of his parables we find him urgently trying to communicate in this way his most central belief about the kingdom.

What was this belief? We see it very clearly if we remind ourselves what Judaism had traditionally thought about the kingdom of God. The Jews felt that a hard-and-fast line separated them from it. At present the kingdom existed strictly in another world, where God was in his glory. One day, perhaps soon, that glorious kingdom would come to earth. When it did arrive, only the righteous people in Israel would be admitted to it. This meant that Israelites must in the meantime try to achieve that righteousness by keeping the Law.

Jesus did not think in these terms at all. Certainly he did not doubt that the kingdom would one day come to earth. Almost certainly he expected it to happen soon. But this future coming of the kingdom – which was after all a long-standing feature of Jewish hopes – was his *presupposition* rather than his *message.* His message was a call to decision, a call to men to repent of their sins, a call to them not merely to keep the Law but to meet the universal and total demands that God was making of them. This was the message, and it gained its tremendous urgency – an urgency that can be seen in all his teachings – because he believed that the kingdom of God might come to earth at any moment, and that there was no possible way in which men could understand its workings. Jewish tradition had regarded the kingdom as something whose nature could be understood or at least guessed at by men, something almost *predictable.* Jesus totally rejected this. He told his hearers that they must regard the kingdom as something utterly and totally mysterious.

This can be understood more easily if we look at some examples. Jewish writers in late Old Testament and early Christian times were fond of picturing the coming of the kingdom of God in terms like this, taken from the book of Ezra, not in the Bible:

> Suddenly the sun will shine by night and the moon by day. From the trees will drip blood, stones will cry out. The nations will fall into tumult, the heavenly regions into chaos; and there shall come to power one whom dwellers on earth expect not. The birds fly away, the sea of Sodom brings forth fish, and roars at night with a voice, which many do not understand, though all hear. At many places the abyss opens, fire bursts forth and blazes long, then the wild beasts forsake their haunts. Women bear monsters, in fresh water salt is found.

It is true that this sort of prophecy of the end is found on Jesus's lips in the apocalyptic discourses before the Passion (Mark chapter 13, Matthew chapter 24, Luke chapter 21). But the argument for regarding these discourses as not authentic is very strong. Much more characteristic of Jesus elsewhere in the Gospels is this warning to his hearers not to indulge in this sort of speculation:

The Pharisees asked him, 'When will the kingdom of God come?' He said, 'You cannot tell by observation when the kingdom of God comes. There will be no saying, "Look, here it is!" or "there it is"; for in fact the kingdom of God is among you.' (Lk. 17. 20–1)

These last words might be taken by an incautious commentator to mean that 'the kingdom of God' was not a supernatural power but an inward spiritual state in men. It would be less misleading to render the original Greek as: 'for in fact the kingdom of God is [suddenly] in your midst'—in other words, the kingdom will suddenly come upon you when you least expect it. For this is Jesus's view of the kingdom. He sees it as something not at all to be described in normal terms, but as thoroughly unpredictable, unknowable, other-worldly and miraculous:

The kingdom of God is like this. A man scatters seed on the land; he goes to bed at night and gets up in the morning, and the seed sprouts and grows – how, he does not know. (Mk. 4. 26–7)

'How, he does not know': to the first-century mind there can have been few things more mysterious than the germination and sprouting of a seed. As the celebrated theologian Rudolf Bultmann reminds us:

Such a parable must not be read in the light of the modern conceptions of 'nature' and 'evolution'. The parable presupposes that the growth and ripening of the seed is not something 'natural', within Man's control, but that it is something miraculous. As the grain springs up miraculously and ripens without human agency or understanding, so marvellous is the coming of the Kingdom of God.

The same message is found in other parables of the kingdom:

How shall we picture the kingdom of God, or by what parable shall we describe it? It is like the mustard-seed, which is smaller than any seed in the ground at its sowing. But once sown, it springs up and grows taller than any other plant, and forms branches so large that the birds can settle in its shade. (Mk. 4. 30–2; cf. Matt. 13. 31–2, Lk. 13. 18–19)

The kingdom of Heaven is like yeast, which a woman took and mixed with half a hundredweight of flour till it was all leavened. (Matt. 13.33)

There are few things stranger to the unscientific mind than the workings of yeast, which mysteriously and relentlessly alters the nature of an entire lump of dough. Just so will the kingdom come to earth – in a way which cannot be understood or foretold by men.

And because the coming of the kingdom could not be foretold, because its nature was wholly incomprehensible and miraculous, men must not remain idle a moment longer. It might not come, of course, for a long time: we should not suppose that Jesus would necessarily have been disconcerted had he learnt that nearly two thousand years after his lifetime the 'coming' had still not happened. As he himself is reported to have said, no one, not even he, could predict it. It was not in fact the actual *event* of the coming of the kingdom that concerned him. The dramatic happenings which would accompany its arrival did not interest him, nor did he speculate as to what the kingdom would in itself be like. The kingdom concerned him because its coming presented man with a call to decision, a call to repent and be saved. 'The kingdom of God is at hand; *repent*, and believe the good news.'

The news that the kingdom is imminent is of course good, but it is also a demand that men face up to the huge, unlimited, total moral demands which God is making of them. They must mend their lives *now*. Hence the urgency of Jesus's call to the disciples: 'Follow me.' There is simply no time to be lost. So it is that the kingdom, while it may be an entirely future event, acts on men at the present moment, determining the nature of their lives now. A sense of urgency, a need to prepare, to be ready, must be communicated to everyone. As Jesus himself expresses it according to Mark:

> Keep awake, then, for you do not know when the master of the house is coming. Evening or midnight, cock-crow or early dawn – if he comes suddenly, he must not find you asleep. And what I say to you, I say to everyone: Keep awake. (Mk. 13. 35–7)

7 'I have come to set fire to the earth'

If Jesus had not died by crucifixion in Jerusalem, his teaching might well have been forgotten. The Christian Church grew up because Jesus was executed – and because his followers believed that after his death he came back to life again. So, though this book is mainly concerned with the ideas of Jesus, we need to conclude by looking at the events leading up to his death and supposed resurrection, and to ask, what kind of influence did Jesus finally come to exert, both over Christian believers and over non-believers?

Jesus's ministry was apparently first conducted in his home district around Nazareth. Later he seems to have gone further afield in Galilee, but even then he preached only in country places and avoided cities such as Tiberias, apparently setting up a temporary home in the small town of Capernaum on the shore of the Lake of Galilee (see Matt. 4. 13). He seems to have taken care that his words should reach the ears of those whom society thought of as outcasts: blind beggars, people subject to epileptic fits (who were regarded with fear and horror because they were thought to be possessed by demons), and even lepers, who were banished by Law from all normal human contact. It was apparently to such as these, rather than to the affluent who were the mainstay of Judaism, that he directed his mission. As he is reported to have declared: 'It is not the healthy that need a doctor, but the sick' (Mk. 2. 17).

The essence of his message, as we have seen, was an urgent call to repentance, a call to meet the universal and total demands that God was making. It was an urgent message because Jesus believed that the wholly miraculous and incomprehensible kingdom of God might dawn at any moment. It was not in any sense a gentle message, because the demands being made on his hearers were immense. But it was also, at least by implication, a message of love, for to those who accepted the call to repentance and tried to meet God's demands, salvation would be complete. In this sense the message was truly a 'Gospel', 'good news'. And this love which God gave to men who repented was shown in the works of healing which Jesus performed. The healings were in this sense symbolic in that they were acts of forgiveness; the removal of sickness and infirmity signified the casting out of sin. Before healing a paralysed man Jesus says to him: 'My son, your sins are forgiven' (Mk. 2. 5).

The consequence of all this was that man, in the message of Jesus, was brought into a new relationship with God. This relationship was to be one of direct contact. Traditionally, as we have seen, Judaism feared the very name of Yahweh and used it only rarely; 'the Lord' was the usual way of referring to the deity. But to Jesus, Yahweh seemed less like a lord than a father, and this was how he began to talk about him and pray to him:

Whoever does the will of my heavenly Father . . . (Matt. 12. 50)

Father, thy name be hallowed . . . (Lk. 11. 2)

The Gospels record that the actual word he used to address God was *Abba* (Mk. 14. 36), an Aramaic term for 'Father'. And he was explicit in telling his followers that this was how they too must address God:

When you pray, go into a room by yourself, shut the door, and pray to your Father who is there in the secret place . . . This is how you should pray: 'Our Father in heaven, thy name be hallowed; thy kingdom come, thy will be done, on earth as in heaven . . .'. (Matt. 6. 6, 9–10)

As to the geographical limits of his mission, Jesus apparently restricted his work to Jewish soil, for his whole message was based on Judaism. There is no reason to suppose that he did not share the belief of his contemporaries that the kingdom of God, when it came to earth, would be peopled first and foremost by the chosen Israelites; 'Gentiles' or non-Jews would play only a secondary part in it. Later, when there existed a Christian Church that was no longer exclusively Jewish, the Gospels tried to suggest that Jesus had made at least brief journeys into the Gentile territories surrounding Galilee, and that he had even preached in Samaria, whose inhabitants, though their religion was related to Judaism, were held in deep suspicion by the Jews (see e.g. Mk 7. 24 ff., Jn. 4. 4 ff.). But Matthew was probably nearer the truth when he recorded Jesus as saying to his disciples: 'Do not take the road to Gentile lands, and do not enter any Samaritan town; but go rather to the lost sheep of the house of Israel' (Matt. 10. 5–6).

Though Jesus preached first of all in Galilee, it was imperative, if he was to make more than a purely local impact on Judaism, that he take his message to Jerusalem, the capital of

Judaea and also the seat of the temple, the only place where the full sacrificial cult of Yahweh could be practised – for sacrifice was never offered in the provincial synagogues, which were simply meeting-houses for prayer and readings. Moreover it was in Jerusalem that the great scribal schools such as those of Shammai and Hillel were established; and it was to Jerusalem that thousands of pilgrims came several times a year for the great Jewish religious festivals. Moreover, during the Galilean stage of his ministry Jesus had almost certainly met opposition from representatives of the established sects of Judaism, especially the Pharisees, and he may have wanted to face that opposition in full force in Jerusalem.

Mark and the other Synoptics would have us believe that at every stage of his preaching and healing work in Galilee his steps were dogged by 'Scribes and Pharisees' who voiced their disapproval of his message and behaviour. We are unlikely to accept this as historically very accurate; little is known about the extent to which the Pharisaic movement and its scribal experts penetrated and influenced Galilean Judaism in the first century, but it seems improbable that its representatives should have been at hand with quite such regularity to comment chorus-fashion on the words and deeds of Jesus. They come in pat on cue in a way which resembles a stage play rather than real life. But we should not assume from this that no kind of Pharisaic opposition to Jesus had materialised in Galilee. If his success was anything like as great as the Gospels report, he would have quickly been seen as a challenge to established Judaism in general and probably to the Pharisees' scrupulous observance of the oral tradition of the Law in particular. Jesus may in fact have seemed to be yet one more example of the anti-Pharisaic element which was already present in Judaism. While many Pharisees were undoubtedly good and worthy men, their insistence on scrupulous observance of the oral Law was regarded, at least in some circles, as hypocrisy; a contemporary text speaks of them as men whose 'hands and hearts were busy with uncleanness and whose mouth did speak proud things, and who said, Draw not near me lest you defile me!' Whether Jesus himself made similarly critical remarks about the Pharisees we cannot say for certain, but the Gospels certainly record him as doing so:

Alas for you Pharisees! You pay tithes of mint and rue and every garden-herb, but have no care for justice and the love of God. It is these you should have practised, without neglecting the others . . . you lawyers [i.e. Scribes], it is no better with you! For you load men with intolerable burdens, and will not put a single finger to the load. (Lk. 11. 42, 46)

Whether or not Jesus spoke in these actual terms, they certainly represent the character of his message, and the Pharisaic party and its Scribes must have regarded him as a radical challenge.

Undoubtedly therefore he went to Jerusalem knowing both that he would be able to preach to a wider audience, and that he would meet opposition. It is indeed not impossible that he actually foresaw arrest and execution. There was a certain tradition in Judaism of the voice of prophecy being suddenly and violently silenced; prophets had been executed and otherwise persecuted, and one had even been stoned to death in the court of the temple itself. So, even if we do not accept the very explicit Gospel predictions by Jesus of his trial and death, we may imagine that 'he set his face resolutely towards Jerusalem' (Lk. 9. 51) with a distinct awareness that he might have some sort of ordeal to undergo. Perhaps most of all he was anxious to communicate his vital message to the whole of Judaism before, as he feared and expected, he was forcibly made silent. As Jesus himself expresses it in Luke's Gospel (12. 49–50), 'I have come to set fire to the earth, and how I wish it were already kindled! I have a baptism to undergo, and what constraint I am under until the ordeal is over!'

Jerusalem: trial and death

It is possible (as John's Gospel in fact alleges) that Jesus made not one but a series of visits to Jerusalem; at all events, his work certainly ended there. The Gospel accounts of his activities in the city are extremely bare, but it is clear that he preached in the temple, and had a series of encounters with the Pharisees and the Sadducees.

The Pharisees were not the conservatives of Jerusalem. Indeed, with their emphasis on the oral rather than the written Law, and with their belief in such things as the resurrection of the dead, they were comparatively almost radical. The real conservatives were the Sadducees (the meaning of whose name is obscure), who accepted only the written Law and rejected the oral tradition, and did not believe in immortality. At the time of Jesus they were the ruling party, having a majority on the Sanhedrin (the parliamentary judicial council) and wielding considerable power under the Romans. They were opposed to any political ferment among the populace, which they saw as a threat not merely to the Romans but to their own authority.

The Gospels record a few disputes between Jesus and the Pharisees and Sadducees in Jerusalem. The Sadducees question him about his views on immortality and resurrection (Mk. 12. 18–24), and the Pharisees ask him an awkward question about whether Jews should pay taxes to Rome (Mk. 12. 14–15). In both cases his answers are ingenious but evasive; it appears that he did not wish to be drawn into a debate. He also avoids giving any direct answer to the question, put to him by the religious authorities, 'By what authority are you acting like this?' (Mk. 11. 28). He replies:

> I have a question to ask you too; and if you give me an answer, I will tell you by what authority I act. The baptism of John: was it from God, or from men? Answer me. (Mk. 11. 29–30)

The questioners are unable to give a judicious answer, and are silenced.

We may suggest that such disputes were in fact more numerous and protracted than the Gospels suggest, and that in Jerusalem Jesus faced a serious challenge to his authority and message from the established religious factions, who united temporarily for the purpose. As to his teaching in the city, no substantial account is preserved, and we have only brief glimpses of him 'teaching the people in the temple and telling them the good news' (Lk. 20. 1). What interests the Gospel writers much more is his attitude to the temple itself.

All four Gospels record that he went into the outer courtyard of the temple and drove out the traders and money changers who had stalls there. They also report that this incident was violent in character; Mark says he 'upset the tables' (11. 15) and John that he 'made a whip of cords and drove them out' (2. 15). The implication is that he objected to the secularisation of the temple; but it is not very clear why he should do so, for the traders were there solely to sell commodities needed for sacrifice, while the money changers exchanged Greek and Roman coins for the Jewish currency required for payment of the temple dues. We can draw no definite conclusions. It is of course possible that Jesus publicly attacked, in some form or other, the whole nature and function of the temple. That he should do so would not be very surprising. Sacrifices were controlled by minutely detailed regulations, and he might have expressed impatience with the notion that this sort of practice was *enough* as a way of worshipping God. There is also the accusation reportedly made in his trial that he had said: 'I will pull down the temple, made with human hands, and in three days I will build another, not made with hands.' (Mk. 14. 58). This is overlaid with a prediction of Jesus's own resurrection after three days, and in that form we may regard it as improbable. But it seems possible that behind it there lies some real attack made by Jesus on the temple.

Was Jesus, during his time in Jerusalem, publicly identified as the Messiah? All four Gospels record that his entry into the city was accompanied by the acclamations of a crowd who hailed him as Messiah; even John, who usually ignores the political implications of Jesus's role, records that they cried 'God bless the king of Israel!' (Jn. 12. 13). We may suspect that, whatever Jesus's own wish to dissociate himself from political claims, he was being increasingly identified with the hoped-for national Messiah who would free Israel from Roman rule. This would certainly help to explain the authorities' concern to suppress him.

The Synoptic Gospels say that Jesus, knowing very well that he was about to be arrested, presided over a meal attended by his twelve disciples, at which he instituted the breaking and eating of bread and the sharing of a cup of wine (as a 'New Covenant'), which afterwards became the central rite of the Christian Church. The precise historicity of this 'Last Supper' cannot be determined, and not all commentators accept that Jesus meant there to be any special ritual meaning in his actions. But this meal was certainly a part of the tradition about Jesus from the earliest days; it is one of the very few details of Jesus's life which Paul mentions to his readers (1 Cor. 11. 23–6), and some event almost certainly took place. Indeed, if we assume that Jesus suspected that his arrest was near, it would be natural that he should wish to conclude his ministry in some formal fashion. He may simply have wished to institute a symbolic meal which was to remind men of the close 'communion' with God which he had always emphasised in his ministry. Or if, as seems likely, he saw his twelve disciples as the patriarchs of a 'new Israel' – twelve was the number of the legendary tribes of ancient Israel – he may indeed have wished to make a new form of Covenant between God and his chosen people. Whether he really saw the bread and wine as in some sense his own body and blood (as the Gospels say he did) cannot be determined.

It is not at all clear from the Gospels on what grounds Jesus was arrested. The implication seems to be that the authorities had no particular charge in mind but were determined to silence him at all costs, and intended to trump up accusations when he was in custody. This seems somewhat unlikely in view of the detailed rules which governed Jewish judicial procedure, and (bearing in mind that the Law expressly forbade 'false witness') it is hard to accept the Gospel picture of a string of witnesses extravagantly and inefficiently perjuring themselves in order to get Jesus convicted. In fact the Gospels say that grounds of conviction were not found until he himself claimed, during the trial, to be the Son of Man who would come on the clouds of heaven – an unambiguous reference to the book of Daniel. We have already seen that there are reasons to doubt that Jesus made such a claim on this occasion; nor, if he did, was it technically blasphemy (a cursing of the divine name), so that one may wonder if it would have been enough to condemn him to death. In these and many other particulars the Gospel accounts of the judicial proceedings against Jesus are unsatisfactory and puzzling.

In fact the part that the Romans played in the proceedings is likely to have been greater than the Gospels indicate. That Jesus was executed by crucifixion indicates that it was beyond doubt the Romans who actually put him to death – it was the Roman method of capital punishment at the time: the Jews, when they were allowed to execute criminals, practised stoning. It is indeed possible that the Jews may have played no part at all in Jesus's arrest, trial and death. If he was being publicly acclaimed in Jerusalem at festival time as 'king of the Jews', the Romans may have regarded this as a sign of political insurgence, and may have decided that a summary execution was the best way of dealing with it. This is borne out by the words fixed by the Romans over Jesus's cross during his execution, words which indicated the charge against him: 'The king of the Jews' (Mk. 15. 26 and parallels). As to why the Gospels shifted the blame from the Romans to the Jews, this can be explained by the fact that Christianity in its first centuries was very much under the shadow of the Roman Empire, and did its best to minimise the grounds for conflict with Rome; moreover after the Jewish wars of the mid-first century the Jews were disgraced in the eyes of the Empire. There is also the fact that quite early in its history the Christian Church split with Judaism, and came to regard it with hostility. From this it was perhaps only a short step to blaming the Jews for Jesus's death. On the other hand it should be noted that the Gospel emphasis on the part played in Jesus's death by the Jewish religious leaders is so strong that it is hard to dismiss it entirely. Moreover the small detail of Peter waiting in the High Priest's courtyard during the trial (Mk. 14. 53 ff.) indicates, at least to those who believe that Peter's reminiscences played some part in shaping the Gospel traditions, that there were Jewish judicial proceedings against Jesus.

So we do not know precisely who was responsible for Jesus's arrest, trial and execution; nor do we know what was in his mind as he went to his death. Those who hold that he identified himself with the Suffering Servant believe that he regarded his suffering as an atonement for the sins of men; those who do not will make no such claim for him. But we can be reasonably certain that he regarded his death as having some positive bearing on his message. He had, after all, preached that the demands of God were utterly uncompromising. Clearly he believed that those demands should be met even if the result were persecution and death. Perhaps there was also in his mind the realisation that by dying – especially by dying the death of a criminal – he was taking to its ultimate limit the willingness to place himself among social outcasts that had always marked his mission. Whether he expected to return to life again after he had died, or envisaged a glorious 'coming' back to earth as Son of Man in the Daniel sense, we do not know. Such ideas are certainly not incongruous with his belief in the miraculous nature of the kingdom of God.

As to the execution itself, the Gospel account of it is largely written to show how in its details it fulfilled Old Testament prophecies. Passages from Psalms 22 and 69 (poetic cries of dereliction) and from Isaiah chapter 53 (the Suffering Servant) have been woven into the narrative so as to demonstrate that everything took place 'according to the Scriptures'. There is little to suggest that Jesus's disciples were able to give any real first-hand report of what happened, and indeed the probability is that by this time they were in hiding, frightened, desolate, and themselves in fear of execution. Bearing this in mind, it is all the more remarkable that they soon came to believe that Jesus was no longer dead but had been raised to life again by God.

The resurrection

Quite apart from the physical possibility of a resurrection, which must remain a matter for belief or disbelief, many commentators find the Gospel accounts of Jesus's appearances to his disciples after his death extremely hard to accept on grounds of internal consistency and logic, let alone the very puzzling fact that Mark's Gospel (apparently the earliest) comes to an end so abruptly and inconclusively with the description of the frightened women leaving the empty tomb. Moreover there is no reason to assume without question that the detail of the empty tomb, on which the story largely depends, was an early part of the resurrection tradition. Paul makes no mention of it in his account of the resurrection (1 Cor. 15. 3ff.), an account which he introduces as 'the facts which had been imparted to me', and which therefore probably predates the Gospels by at least twenty years. The Gospels say that Joseph of Arimathaea, a rich Jew, obtained the body with Pilate's permission and buried it in his own tomb, but this might be legend. Jesus could have been buried not in any marked grave but in some common burial ground for criminals, so that there was no tomb to be found empty.

On the other hand we must realise that to reject the Gospel accounts of the resurrection and to explain what happened as an experience in the minds of Jesus's disciples presents its own difficulties. It was certainly a very remarkable thing if a group (probably a small group) of frightened men could change its mind and believe that what had appeared to be final defeat was in fact victory. Certainly there are many other instances in history of celebrated persons being supposed to be alive after their death. Such a thing, for example, was often believed of Hitler and other exceptionally evil men, the force of whose personality was so great that the news of their death was simply not accepted by many people. But this is not the same as belief in a resurrection.

Nor can the belief in the resurrection be explained, as can many things in the Gospels, as a 'fulfilment of prophecy'; for no such thing had been prophesied. Certainly the Servant Songs declared that God would raise his Servant from the dead and would restore him to bodily life, so that he would 'enjoy long life and see his children's children' (Is. 53. 10), but this was not at all what was being claimed for Jesus. Indeed when the early Church began to preach that Jesus had risen from the dead on the Sunday morning after his death it had some difficulty in making it seem that the Old Testament really had foretold that such a thing would happen. The nearest text that could be found to a prophecy of such a resurrection was Hosea 6. 2: '... after two days he will revive us, on the third day he will restore us, that in his presence we may live'. The truth is that, as the theologian C. F. Evans puts it, 'Resurrection is certainly not something which could have been arrived at by reflection on the Old Testament.'

Those who regard mythology as having a profound influence

on human thought will look for a different source for the resurrection belief. From them comes the suggestion that it grew from the ancient notion of the Dying and Rising God, a figure found in early mythologies, including those of Egypt, Mesopotamia, and pre-Jewish Palestine itself. Traces of this figure can (it has been argued) even be found in the Old Testament. But it is hard to imagine how this mythological notion might have had a practical effect on the minds of Jesus's disciples at this moment of crisis.

The historian who does not believe in the resurrection will conclude that the belief in it grew up because of a spontaneous change of mind by the disciples, a decision by them that Jesus was not dead after all. But, even if this is the explanation, one thing must not be missed. Such a belief about Jesus is the most enormous tribute to the force of his personality in his lifetime.

The Lord Jesus Christ

The result of this belief in the resurrection was that a new religion grew up, centred on the person of Jesus. 'Christianity', as it soon came to be called, was not simply a religion which incorporated his teachings; it was a religion *about* him, and about his death and resurrection in particular. It declared that these events were a special self-revelation of God in the field of history, that they had atoned for the sins of mankind, and that all who believed in God and in his Son 'the Lord Jesus Christ' could attain eternal life in God's kingdom. It was a religion of salvation, and Jesus's actual teachings in Galilee and Judaea were only one aspect of his importance as the central figure in it. 'Jesus saves' was the message of Christianity, and his death and resurrection were the chief events by which this was believed to have happened. As Paul expressed it, '... if Christ was not raised, then our Gospel is null and void' (1 Cor. 15. 14).

It would seem very much as if this Gospel of Paul and other early Christians was markedly different from the 'good news' that Jesus preached during his ministry. Indeed many theologians believe that Paul and other early Christian preachers were the true founders of Christianity, in that it was they rather than Jesus himself who constructed a religion around his person. How true this is depends, of course, on our view of Jesus. But if we do not regard him exclusively as a teacher, and accept that he admitted (if only tacitly) the claims of his disciples that he was God's special agent, then we must allow some measure of continuity between Jesus and the early Church.

It is very difficult to assess the exact degree to which the historical Jesus influenced Paul and other early preachers. Certainly it appears from his letters that Paul was not greatly concerned to base his own teachings on what Jesus had taught. He felt he was being guided by Jesus as the living Lord, not by the specific sayings of the Jesus who had walked in Palestine. In fact he often departs dramatically from Jesus's teachings; for example, instead of demanding that his congregations should sell all that they possessed and give to the poor he wrote: 'There is no question of relieving others at the cost of hardship to yourselves' (2 Cor. 8. 14). On the other hand Paul's letters are addressed to those already instructed in the Christian faith, and we cannot say for certain how much new converts would have been told about the actual life and teachings of Jesus. Moreover it would be hard to imagine that the Gospels were written in a climate of declining interest in Jesus himself; they seem to indicate rather the opposite.

Nevertheless there was undoubtedly a tendency in the early Church to centre Christian faith not so much on what Jesus *had* done during his earthly ministry but on the salvation he could offer to Christians *now*. Early preachers spoke of the glorious Jesus of the present – and of the future, since the Church confidently expected his return 'on the clouds of heaven' to judge the living and the dead and to inaugurate God's kingdom on earth. Paul wrote of the day

> when our Lord Jesus Christ is revealed from heaven with his mighty angels in blazing fire. Then he will do justice upon those who refuse to acknowledge God and upon those who will not obey the gospel of our Lord Jesus. They will suffer the punishment of eternal ruin, cut off from the presence of the Lord and the splendour of his might, when on that great Day he comes to be glorified among his own and adored among all believers . . . (2 Thess. 1. 7–10)

Paul, at least at first, expected that the 'great Day' would happen in his own lifetime; early in his work as a preacher he talked of 'we who are left alive until the Lord comes' (1 Thess. 4. 15). But the years passed and the glorious event did not occur; and, though the Church never abandoned the hope of Jesus's Second Coming – it believes in it still – it began to shift the emphasis of its teaching away from this hope for the future, and more towards the belief that Jesus could offer salvation to believers *now*. One result of this change of emphasis was John's Gospel, which, much more than the Synoptics, emphasises Jesus's role as Saviour of the world. It is possible to see in the Synoptic picture of Jesus, despite the many problems of the narrative, a historical person. John shows us not a Jesus of history but the Word of God made flesh, the saving Christ whose call is to all who believe in him: 'I am the light of the world. No follower of mine shall wander in the dark; he shall have the light of life' (Jn. 8. 12).

From this point onwards until modern times it becomes virtually impossible to distinguish the influence of Jesus himself from the influence of Christianity. Up to the nineteenth century Jesus's message was only perceived through the medium of the Church. Even the Reformation, which challenged established ideas about the Church's authority, returned not to the specific teachings of the historical Jesus but to the Pauline theology of personal salvation through Jesus as Lord. Until the beginnings of modern historical research the distinction was not really made beween the ideas *of* Jesus himself – his actual teaching – and ideas *about* him, by which is meant Christianity's belief in him as Saviour.

Indeed at certain periods in the Church's history it can be said that the followers of Jesus drastically misinterpreted his teachings or overlaid them with views of their own. The Christian belief that salvation was a gift from God and could not be achieved by the works of men led to a a tendency, particularly in the early years of Christianity, to ignore the ethical demands of religion and concentrate on its mystical aspects. As J. L. Houlden puts it:

> As salvation was not to be found in the life and activity of this world but only by escape into a wholly mystical present or an otherworldly future, ethics lost their force and significance. God held the initiative, only God could act in this cause; why then should man concern himself with duties dictated solely by his bodily existence?

This streak of 'antinomianism' or moral lawlessness arose partly because some early Christians misinterpreted the assertion made by such preachers as Paul that Jesus had 'ended' the Law. Antinomianism was, of course, a complete perversion of what Jesus himself had taught: his message was not that God made no ethical demands, but that the demands were total and unlimited, and could not be circumscribed by the Law. In fact antinomianism did not become a dominant feature of Christianity; Paul and his contemporaries took much trouble to oppose it, particularly when it led (as it often did) to sexual licence; see 1 Cor. 6. 12–20, where Paul attacks those who say, in the name of Jesus Christ, 'I am free to do anything.' But the fact that the antinomians could – however erroneously – claim the authority of Jesus for their licentious behaviour shows how much his teaching was subject to misinterpretation.

Nor were such distortions of Jesus's mesage confined to the early Church. At many times in the history of Christianity there have been sects of believers who have regarded scrupulous moral purity as being of paramount importance for salvation – the exact opposite, in fact, of antinomianism; and again this has been done in the name of Jesus. The Puritans of seventeenth-century England are a particularly obvious example of this, and something of the kind can also be found in those present-day 'evangelical' Christians, especially in the United States, who regard abstinence from tobacco and alcohol as a *sine qua non* of faith in Jesus. Needless to say, there is no evidence that the historical Jesus endorsed such attitudes, which resemble those of the Pharisees rather than that of Jesus himself and his followers.

It may be objected that these are extremes, and that within the central stream of Christianity the message of Jesus remains largely unimpaired. This may be so, and certainly the Gospels are read at every celebration of the 'Lord's Supper', so that in this central act of worship Christians are constantly reminded of the sayings and actions of Jesus himself, at least as the Gospels recorded them. On the other hand it cannot be said that the Church concerns itself very much to emphasise the radical character of Jesus's ethical teachings. What matters to it is Jesus's power to save *now*: he is the living Lord, rather than just a historical figure on whose teachings the Church is based. This means that his influence on his followers is quite different from that of Muhammad or Gautama, the teachers – and they claimed to be no more than teachers – who founded Islam and Buddhism.

If we ask what has been the influence of Jesus outside the Christian Church, the question is very difficult to answer. Certainly there have been occasions when Christian ethics – and thus perhaps ultimately the teachings of Jesus – have shaped world events. Slavery was eventually abolished in Western society in the nineteenth century largely as a result of pressure from Christians. On the other hand the early and medieval Church supported slavery as an institution – 'Slaves, give entire obedience to your earthly masters' wrote Paul (Col. 3. 22) – and it may be said in general that Christianity has often been content to accept the moral *status quo* of its time, only changing its moral outlook as society itself does so.

In the humanities and the arts the figure of Jesus has certainly been of great importance. From early and medieval times until very recently the great majority of European moral thinkers and artists often drew in one way or another on Christian beliefs. Works as diverse as Dante's *Divine Comedy* and Bach's *St Matthew Passion*, as well as whole schools of European religious painting, testify to the imaginative appeal of Jesus and of the Church who worshipped him. Yet it can scarcely be said that this reflects the intellectual achievement of the historical Jesus. Here too it is Jesus as Saviour, as the central figure in a religion of salvation, that has caught hold of men's minds.

Now the picture has changed, and the decline of religious belief in many areas of Western society, together with the increase of historical research into the events behind the Gospels, means that the influence of Jesus is today rather different. Outside the Church, Jesus sometimes appears as a figurehead for movements which profess no religious belief about him, but are attracted by what they regard as his anti-establishment message of love and compassion. To them he appeals because (they say) he rejected fixed rules and attacked moral hypocrisy. Such an interpretation of Jesus is dubious to say the least; though he was certainly a radical, he opposed not established society in general but specific religious abuses of his day, and while he preached love and compassion he balanced this with enormous moral demands; nor did he reject moral rules so much as declare them to be inadequate. It has to be said that modern movements of this kind which claim to follow the message of Jesus are not really doing so at all. Meanwhile within Christianity there is a steadily increasing tendency, at least in radical quarters, to reject the whole supernatural framework of religion as mythical, not literally true, and this has been accompanied by an attempt to posit some other kind of philosophical system in which the teachings of Jesus, 'de-mythologised', might make sense. In particular, existentialism has been offered by many theologians as an alternative to the old Judaeo–Christian picture of God, Heaven and Hell; and this existential interpretation of Jesus and Christianity is at present finding wide acceptance in theological circles. It must be said, however, that it has largely failed to communicate itself to those not acquainted with the intricacies of modern philosophy, and it certainly lacks the direct, immediate, and ultimately *simple* character of the message of Jesus himself.

It is because of this simplicity of his teaching that Jesus has, despite all the confusions and perversions of his message over the centuries, continued to have a powerful influence on the human mind. He was not a philosopher; he did not construct any complete system of ethics; nor did he speak in moral abstractions which can be straightforwardly detached from the context of his religious beliefs. But in the manner of his teaching, his refusal to compromise when faced with any moral dilemma, his emphasis on the universality and totality, the unlimitedness of moral demands on men, there is a force which crosses all religious barriers and appeals to us whether or not we subscribe to his religious beliefs. This, we feel instinctively, is how moral problems should be attacked. We may find that in practice it is often impossible to do so; and certainly he taught in hyperbole. Yet despite the inconsistencies in his teaching, despite the fact that it was never designed as a detailed rule for daily life, it has a sharpness and immediacy which makes the teaching of almost every other moralist (however sane and wise and well balanced) seem pale by comparison. Jesus was not just a moral teacher: this book has tried to emphasise that fact. His appeal was just as much charismatic as intellectual. But in the field of moral teaching his forcefulness has had no equal.

Sources and further reading

Among the many modern translations of the Bible, *The New English Bible* (Oxford University Press and Cambridge University Press, 1970) is particularly recommended. Those who wish to study the original Greek of the New Testament will find a number of editions available, among them one which prints a literal English translation between the lines of the Greek; this is *The R. S. V. Interlinear Greek-English New Testament* (Samuel Bagster & Sons Ltd., 1958).

There are many modern commentaries on the Gospels. These vary greatly both in the viewpoint of the commentator and the detail into which they go. The Pelican New Testament Commentaries provide a good cross-section of modern opinion, and that on Mark's Gospel by D. E. Nineham (Penguin, 1963) has been invaluable in the writing of this book. A more conservative view of Mark and of the reliability of the Gospels in general is taken by V. Taylor in *The Gospel According to St Mark* (Macmillan, 1953); his commentary is worth studying both for this and for the great detail in which he examines the original Greek. Matthew's Gospel is perhaps best studied with the aid of the commentary by H. Benedict Green (New Clarendon Bible, Oxford University Press, 1975), and John's Gospel with the aid of the commentary by Barnabas Lindars (New Century Bible, Oliphants, 1972). There are many commentaries on Luke, of which one of the best is still that by J. M. Creed (Macmillan, 1930).

Studies of Jesus and the New Testament are so numerous that only a very few of those available can be mentioned here. The following books are included simply because they were a help to the present writer. *A Short History of Religions* by E. E. Kellett (Penguin, 1962) provides an admirable survey of religions in the ancient world, while John Bright's *A History of Israel* (S.C.M. Press, 1972) and Bo Reicke's *The New Testament Era* (A. & C. Black, 1969) give a good summary of the historical background to Christianity. The teachings of the rabbis Hillel and Shammai, whose work has been contrasted in this book with the teaching of Jesus, are found in the *Mishnah*, translated by Herbert Danby (Oxford University Press, 1933). As regards Jesus himself, two of the best books on the character of his teaching and of his ministry in general are Rudolf Bultmann's *Jesus and the Word* (Fontana, 1958) and H. J. Cadbury's *Jesus: What Manner of Man?* (Macmillan, 1947), while J. L. Houlden's *Ethics and the New Testament* (Mowbrays, 1975) is a useful summary of the difficulties of disentangling what Jesus really taught, and of the moral differences between the authors of the different New Testament books. On the subject of Jesus's messianic claims and the background to those claims, S. Mowinckel's *He That Cometh* (Blackwell, 1959) is the best summary of the traditional view, while the more radical view that Jesus meant nothing extraordinary by his use of the term 'son of man' is argued by Geza Vermes in *Jesus the Jew* (Fontana, 1976), a book which is full of fascinating detail about the Jewish background to Jesus's ministry. The trial and death of Jesus are discussed fully in John Knox's *The Death of Christ* (Collins, 1959); on this subject see also *Roman Society and Roman Law in the New Testament* by A. N. Sherwin-White (Clarendon Press, 1963). The resurrection and the problems surrounding the Gospel accounts of it are discussed very usefully in C. F. Evans's *Resurrection and the New Testament* (S.C.M. Press, 1970).

The history of Gospel studies is a subject in itself. The best introduction to it is *The New Testament: the History of the Investigation of its Problems* by W. G. Kümmel (S.C.M. Press, 1973), while Robert Grant's *A Historical Introduction to the New Testament* (Fontana, 1971) is a handy paperback summary of the subject. Recent New Testament studies which have influenced the writing of this book include John Drury's *Tradition and Design in Luke's Gospel* (Darton, Longman & Todd, 1976) and Michael Goulder's *Midrash and Lection in Matthew* (S.P.C.K., 1974). And finally mention must be made again of that fascinating volume by Albert Schweitzer, *The Quest of the Historical Jesus* (3rd edition, A. & C. Black, 1954), with its timely reminder that 'There is no historical task which so reveals a man's true self as the writing of a Life of Jesus.'

Index

Past Masters

AQUINAS Anthony Kenny

Anthony Kenny writes about Thomas Aquinas as a philosopher, for readers who may not share Aquinas's theological interests and beliefs. He begins with an account of Aquinas's life and works, and assesses his importance for contemporary philosophy. The book is completed by more detailed examinations of Aquinas's metaphysical system and his philosophy of mind.

DANTE George Holmes

George Holmes expresses Dante's powerful originality by identifying the unexpected connections the poet made between received ideas and his own experience. He presents Dante's biography both as an expression of the intellectual dilemma of early Renaissance Florence and as an explanation of the poetic, philosophical and religious themes developed in his works. He ends with a discussion of the *Divine Comedy*, Dante's poetic panorama of hell, purgatory and heaven.

HUME A. J. Ayer

A. J. Ayer begins his study of Hume's philosophy with a general account of Hume's life and works, and then discusses his philosophical aims and methods, his theories of perception and self-identity, his analysis of causation, and his treatment of morals, politics and religion. He argues that Hume's discovery of the basis of causality and his demolition of natural theology were his greatest philosophical achievements.

Past Masters

MARX Peter Singer

Peter Singer identifies the central vision that unifies Marx's thought, enabling us to grasp Marx's views as a whole. He views him as a philosopher primarily concerned with human freedom, rather than as an economist or social scientist. He explains alienation, historical materialism, the economic theory of *Capital*, and Marx's idea of communism, in plain English, and concludes with a balanced assessment of Marx's achievement.

PASCAL Alban Krailsheimer

Alban Krailsheimer opens his study of Pascal's life and work with a description of Pascal's religious conversion, and then discusses his literary, mathematical and scientific achievements, which culminated in the acute analysis of human character and powerful reasoning of the *Pensées*. He argues that after his conversion Pascal put his previous work in a different perspective and saw his, and in general all human activity, in religious terms.